THE BEST OF
The Lemon Aid Lady™
Teaching Sweet Successes and Juicy Profits to Party Plan People

Written and Created by
Christie Northrup

Cover design by
Steve James

Published by Lemon Aid Learning Adventures™

Lake Dallas, Texas 75065

Published by Lemon Aid Learning Adventures™

Printed in the United States of America

ISBN: 1-930182-05-8

Dedicated to...

The thousands of loyal Lemon Aid Learners that not only do the Lemon Aid *TWIST*, but who have encouraged others to subscribe to our lively list!

Table of Contents

Introducing The Best of The Lemon Aid Lady

The phone kept ringing. People wanted to buy the *Lead Alphabet* book. Each time I inquired, "Who can I thank for referring you to our company?" the response was "The Internet." Frankly, I was puzzled. This was in the fall of 1998, before I had even thought of building my business with electronic commerce. Since I had no website, how were people finding out about the Lemon Aid Lady?

Through these Lemon Aid Learners, I discovered a valuable information and marketing tool: specific lists for specific groups via the Internet. So, I decided to begin my own list without having any idea of how they worked! I was just eager to share Lemon Aid with thirsty Party Plan People! The list officially began in March 1999.

For the past five years, I've delivered Lemon Aid to the e-mail boxes of thousands of Party Plan People a couple of times each month. On a regular basis, I have requests for past messages that I have posted. Now, you can hold the *Best of the Lemon Aid Lady* messages in your hands and incorporate them into your business.

The first section of the book is organized by the seasons in the calendar. This way, you can refer to specific messages focusing on a particular season. While the messages are organized by calendar, they are not chronological by year. For instance, some of the first messages listed could be some of the most recently written.

The last part of the book is arranged by topic. From understanding Why We Work (www) to discovering a gold mine of customers using Guest Lists, you'll be treated to gallons of ideas. Some of the posts in this section were eventually incorporated in to two of the Lemon Aid books: *Presentations for Profit$* and *Hanging Up on Your Phone Phobias*. While the ideas are similar to what you'll read in those books, the information is not just a "cut and paste." You'll benefit from reading the *TWISTs* from all resources.

To receive all the current Lemon Aid that will quench your thirst for more hosts, customers, recruits, and leaders, visit www.partyplanpeople.com and sign up for the FREE, newly designed Party Plan People newsletter, and invite your team and friends to join as well. You'll want to get every sip!

Chapter One: January—A Time to Begin Anew

Don't Make a Resolution to Call Customers and Prospects

If you've been a subscriber to this Lemon Aid Lady list for a while, you know I send out messages to you often–usually two to three times a month and have done so for nearly five years. I purposely haven't committed to a regular schedule due to my obligations to clients and subsequent travel. And, quite frankly, I sometimes get more inspiration in one month than I do in another.

However, in mid-November, I decided to conduct an experiment, so I pledged a commitment schedule to you, my Lemon Aid Learners. On this schedule, you knew exactly what topic I was going to address on a specific day for the following eight weeks. For the most part, messages were delivered on time. I did have a couple of "Sour Situations" during this period. In the early part of December, I was chosen to serve on a federal jury case, which was emotionally draining, so the message was delayed a couple of days. Last week, while traveling over the holidays, I couldn't access my ISP to send the message; thus, you're getting last week's message today, and the message scheduled for today will be sent next week. So, the commitment is being fulfilled albeit with a *TWIST* in the timing.

At this point, you might think this message is one of explanation. No, it's to illustrate commitment. Because I created my own commitment deadline, or "CD", I followed through and did as I promised by delivering the messages. Throughout this past eight weeks, I had to keep reminding myself that I needed to get the message composed and sent. I kept the schedule in front of me and referred to it often.

Honestly, some weeks I felt I didn't have the time or energy or desire to put it all together (believe it or not, each message takes two to four hours to compose, edit, send, etc.). But I couldn't let myself down. Ah, you might have thought I should have said, "I couldn't let you down." Actually, you might have been disappointed had I not done as committed, and your trust in me might have wavered. But, I am the one who would have been the most disappointed in myself; you might have forgotten I had the schedule, or you might have joined the list after I sent it. But I knew what I had pledged to you and to me and I was committed to that pledge.

Okay, so what does this experience have to do with Hanging up on Phone Phobias—the topic all recent messages have been centered around? It's an illustration of commitment to calling. When you get your copy of the new book the first section in the Lemon Pages tells my story of how I became addicted to calling customers…it began with this commitment to myself. My personal sales and recruiting increased by 25% in one year because of this commitment.

So, as 2004 begins and you want more...or whatever your slogan for the year is, may I suggest you don't make a New Year's resolution to make calls, connect with customers, and hang up on your Phone Phobias...rather, make a commitment. I checked out the dictionary definitions. When you resolve, you come to a definite or earnest decision... when you commit, you make binding obligation, pledge, or assurance. To me, commitment sounds stronger and has more action than simply making a decision. Years ago, I read the following quotation about commitment; unfortunately the author was not listed: "There is a difference between interest and commitment. When you are interested in doing something, you do it only when circumstances permit. When you are committed to something, you accept no excuses, only results!"

In my illustration, I pledged by writing down my plan and told nearly 10,000 people about it–this was my binding obligation, pledge, and assurance. I know, I have one more week to keep my commitment to you; I promise you'll like the preview of some Fun-der-ful ways to connect with your customers, prospects, and team members—fifty of these will be in the new book; two or three will be shared next week on this list.

In 2004, don't make resolutions to call; don't be interested in calling...make a commitment to yourself and D I A L!

On a Roll for January

Are you ready to GET ON A ROLL AND GET YOUR BUSINESS SOAKING WITH SALES? Grab a new (must be new) roll of Bounty® Paper Towels (they're the quicker picker upper and you want to pick up sales/demonstrations/recruits quick!). Each roll probably has 50-100 sheets. Now, start contacting people. As you talk to each person, write her name, phone, and response on one of the sheets of paper towels. DON'T RIP THE TOWELS OFF! Neatly fold the sheets or create another roll (you want to keep them together for the visual effect). See how fast you can use up the whole ROLL, and you'll be on a ROLL! Remember, these names and phone numbers. are worth MILLIONS (if you've been to Presentation$ 4 Profits you know what I mean!). Store them in your Business Bank (See *Deed Alphabet*, pages 18-20). If you need ideas on who to call, refer to the *Lead Alphabet: Where to find customers when you run out of Family and Friends.*

It's a Wonderful Business

As a new year of life and business begins, some of us might be in a Holiday Hang Over Mood (I'm not talking about anything related to alcohol, either). We've taken some time off to enjoy our families and friends and getting back to our business is sometimes a challenge. The sad fact is, January is when many people leave their companies; especially in the companies where you renew your agreements at this time of the year. If you're in the Holiday Hang Over Mood and are questioning why you're doing what you're doing, remember the best Christmas movie of all times: *It's a Wonderful Life*. George Bailey was a hard working, giving man. His life took him in a direction other than what he had planned. Even so, he gave his all to keeping the family business, The Bailey Building and Loan, running. Because of his efforts, many people were able to afford housing, which brought many ripple blessings. Then, he encountered a "Sour Situation." He was hopeless...and decided to take his own life. Fortunately, his guardian angel, Clarence, appeared and gave him a great gift: The ability to see what life would have been without George Bailey.

Before you give up on your business, take some time to think of the people's lives you have influenced and enhanced because you are part of your business. Think of those who you have helped as you've provided your product and your personalized service. Remember the people who now have information to help them provide a better home environment, ways to cook meals and store food, a creative outlet, ideas for preserving memories...and the other extras you provide with one-on-one service relative to your product line. Then, your eyes will really be opened when you look at those you have welcomed into your business at one time or another. Even if some of these people have left the company, surely you gave a part of yourself as you taught them about the industry and gave them unbuyable gifts: confidence, self-esteem, new friends, business education.

And, look at those who are still taking advantage of the opportunity you shared with them. You were the vehicle that introduced them to a better life. Believe me, there have been times when I was ready to commit "business suicide." I wanted to give everything up. Occasionally this was due to my own laziness, disappointments, and discouragement. Other times, jealous people did all in their power to ruin me and my business...like Mr. Potter did to George Bailey. But, as I look over the years that I have recruited, shared, and taught others and also learned from them, I am grateful for what I've given, the lives I have enriched through marketing products, sharing an opportunity, and giving of myself...just as you will realize when you consider, "What difference does it make that I've been in my business?" As *It's a Wonderful Life* ends, George's brother, a war hero, gives George a toast: "To my brother, George: The richest man in town." This is the essence of the entire movie. As you evaluate all the hostesses you have helped, the customers you have contributed to, and the recruits you've raised to a better life, I leave this toast: "To my Lemon Aid Learners...The wealthiest people on earth."

Your Business is a Life Saver

Do you know your business is a lifesaver to you...and others? Yesterday I drove down to Dallas, about 20 miles (one hour of drive time), for a seminar I attended (yes, I too attend seminars!) Driving through the rush hour traffic in both directions made me appreciate how our home-based businesses are a real LIFESAVER because we don't have to fight it!

Then, this afternoon I was at the grocery store and stood in line with a very sharp-looking woman who was holding an adorable, busy little girl. I surmised that the mom was just returning home from work. As we chatted in line (I just had to compliment her on her gorgeous suit; remember, compliments convert casual conversations into committed customers), I found out she would love to have a home based business rather than the grind of the job she has and taking her daughter to a day care (remember, there are millions just like her in your local grocery store!). This mom needs a LIFESAVER!

There are more reasons why your business is a lifesaver...so here's a visual idea to help you find those people. Carry rolls of Five Flavor Lifesaver® Candy around (the small, mini rolls will do). At your presentations, open the roll up, pass it around so everyone can take a lifesaver. Announce that just as you wouldn't eat candy in front of them without sharing with EVERYONE–not just a select few–you want to briefly explain why your business can be a lifesaver for each of them. Then ask:

"Do you feel like you're going in circles, like this candy? You don't know the beginning from the end. Well, here's a lifesaver for each of you! Now ask, who has a YELLOW LIFESAVER? Yellow means I have a BRIGHT BUSINESS...it's a happy environment because I get to teach people like you how to use our products, give gifts to wonderful hostesses, share my business with people who want to work in a bright, happy business, all while helping my family by earning more and being home...

"Speaking of HOME, who has a RED LIFESAVER? Red means LOVE. I love to work from home with the people I LOVE most. And, I also love our products and showing others how to profit from our products by doing presentations. Who has a CLEAR Lifesaver? The reasons for joining my business are CRYSTAL CLEAR, like this Lifesaver: I am home-based and don't have to fight rush hour traffic! (List one or two reasons that makes you and your company really stand out. Perhaps you have terrific incentives like gifts, trips, or automobiles. Do you get paid every week? Can a person begin your business with little or no financial outlay...choose one item that will really grab 'em!) If you're ready to get GOING, the light is GREEN. (See which guests have a green Lifesaver.) Not only does GREEN mean GO, it also stands for $$$$. Now that you know more about how _____ _____ (your company) can be a lifesaver to you, ORANGE you glad you're here to find out more? If so, visit with me after and I'll send you home with your own roll of Lifesavers and we'll discuss more how you can savor your life and business!"

Enjoy this team-building, business-sharing idea!

Let it Snow, Let it Snow, Let it Snow

If you are in an area where you're seeing a lot of white today, tomorrow, and the next day, you'll want to know what SNOW really means: Sell N O W That's right...sell now...right now...today, pick up the phone, you'll probably catch a lot of people home. (Even "shop till you droppers" don't want to be at the mall if it's closed due to SNOW). Today could be "just in time" for you to call and get reorders. For example, if you sell the popular gourmet soup mixes, people are very apt to say "YES...I want a case." You're calling them just in time for them to be thinking about a hot bowl of soup. If you sell something to do with children's activities, call and suggest your "Snow Bound Kit" (a collection that you'll put together for the snow bound days.) If you sell wellness products, extra vitamins to ward off germs or ointments to help with the back muscles strained due to shoveling the white stuff, your products–and phone call–will be Just in Time for many.

Now do the *TWIST* on your own product/service: SNOW CAN ALSO STAND FOR: Show N O W Some of my best demonstrations were in neighborhoods where people had cabin fever, but didn't want to shovel out to go anyplace. As long as you can get there safely (perhaps your own neighborhood), have a SHOP NOW SNOW SHOW (demo, workshop, party)! It's a great chance to meet neighbors who normally are too busy running places. How about those frustrated people who can't get to work, or who don't want to go to work, but their office is open in spite of snow: Sponsor N O W Sponsor (or recruit) them NOW !

As you read this, you might be inclined to turn off your business because of the snow. I'm challenging you to do the Lemon Aid *TWIST* and Sell NOW (SNOW) Show NOW (SNOW) Sponsor NOW (SNOW) That's right, let it SNOW (sell), let it SNOW (show), let it SNOW (sponsor) just in time for your SUCCESS!

Chapter Two: February Holidays

How do You Love Your Business?

Remember when you first began flirting with the idea of beginning your business? Once you made the decision to join, you became engaged with your company. When you received your kit, you were so thrilled; it was like being on a honeymoon with your business. To be sure your business becomes a happily-ever-after enture, do daily business-building activities and NEVER take the opportunity for granted.

Ground Hog Day

Do you all know what today, February 2nd is? Happy Ground Hog Day! According to legend, today is the day when weather for the next six weeks is forecast. The ground hog will wake from its winter nap, come out of the ground, and look around for its shadow. If it sees its shadow, the ground hog will become frightened and go back to sleep for another six weeks of winter. However, if it is an overcast day and the ground hog doesn't see its shadow, this is a sign that spring will be early. (Information found in *World Book Encyclopedia*). What significance does this have on your business? Let's do the *TWIST*:

Today and everyday you forecast the next six weeks of your business. What you do today determines what results and income you have in the next six weeks. Are you still in a winter slumber? Are you going to get up, make a few phone calls, and become frightened because you get a few "no's"? Or, will you come out of your 'hole' and create an early spring (growing season) for your business and life? The ground hog might be afraid of its shadow. However, you will want to go find your shadow today–a new recruit! Today is the perfect day to call that person you've been meaning to call, the one who hasn't decided (fence sitter), the person you met yesterday at lunch, etc. Announce that in celebration of Ground Hog Day, you're looking for your shadow—someone you can teach the business to and share prosperity with. After discovering where they would like to be in their business and life in the next six weeks (by the middle of March), show them what they can accomplish in this short amount of time, when they decide TODAY, to come out of their holes and join your team. So, come out of your hole, look for (don't be afraid of) your shadow, and celebrate the next six weeks of spring and prosperity!

Incorporating all the Festive Red, White, and Heart Items into Your Communications, Demonstrations and Business Opportunity Meetings

I began using simple props because I was gutless when it came to recruiting. I wanted to talk to people about my business, but I didn't know how to begin. If you have similar feelings, read on and put these into action!

Caution: Only use these ideas if you truly LOVE what you do!

Boxes of Conversation Hearts (yes, the kind that have been around since you were in elementary school). Send a box of these (put in a padded envelope) to everyone you want to approach about your business. Put a note in the envelope, "Because you LOVE _____ ____ (company name), we can schedule a HEART-TO-HEART CONVERSATION about joining our business family. I'll be calling you soon!"

Yes, you still need to pick up the phone and set up an appointment.

You can also use these as invitations using the words "Because you LOVE _____ (company name) you are a SWEETHEART and are invited to a HEART-TO-HEART CONVERSATION about joining our business family on (date and time) I'll be calling to tell you the location.

See, if you don't put the location of the event down, you have to pick up the phone and notify her–a great reason to call, which allows you to verbally invite her. Don't depend on this box of hearts to convince someone to join your company or attend an event.

At your demonstrations, pass around a dish of candy hearts. If possible, incorporate your own products into this activity. If you don't have supporting products, call your direct sales friends and purchase their items, or include a spoon and paper cupcake liners so the candy doesn't get messy in the guests' hands.

Ahead of time, you will have chosen a few choice words written on the hearts. See which guest has the most of your chosen words on her hearts. Reward her with a brochure/audio/video/invitation about your business.

Here are the hearts to use. Use the words from a box of conversation hearts (they are readily available) to tell a story or just choose one or two of the lines. The words on the hearts are bold faced:

First Kiss: Do you remember your first kiss? What about your last paycheck? If your paycheck isn't memorable anymore and you're sad every day when you say goodbye to your kids and they say **Miss You** before you get to your car, let's talk. My business could be **For You!** You might not have thought of this before; I didn't, but after I saw **How Sweet** the marketing plan is, I said **I'm sure** this is for me. When I excitedly told my husband/ wife/kids/parents/ about the income possibilities with _____ (company name) they said, "**Get Real!**" They said I must have had a **Dream**. They're right; this is my **Dream** job! Now when I leave to go to work, I have a **Smile** on my face and when I get home, it's even bigger because I meet **Awesome** hosts and guests like you all! In fact, to give you the best service, you can **Write Me**, **Call Me**, or **Fax Me**. Better yet, **Ask Me** today how my business can become the heart of your home!

Another *TWIST*: Instead of reading the story, just offer a special present for anyone who has the "prize" hearts. I'd choose **Ask Me** or **I'm sure** as the "prize" hearts because you want everyone to "ask you" and say "I'm sure" to booking a party or joining your team!

Valentine's Theme Meeting: Refer to "I Love My Business" (Chapter 13) of *Totally Terrific Team Themes* for a fun meeting that will put LOVE and FUN in your team. Available at www.lemonaidlady.com.

In Love with Your Business

Just two weeks until Valentines Day. Here are some fun seasonal ideas for building your business that can be used all year. First, use the "I Love My Business" Theme from the *Totally Terrific Team Themes* book (Chapter 13). You can use this for a team meeting or adapt it for demonstrations.

Next, send a Valentine to all the people in your business bank that asked you to keep in touch with them about joining your business/being a hostess/purchasing your product. Adapt the valentine to your business. Here's an example. I bought the inexpensive children's valentines and added a few words: The card read: "You're a Shoe-in to be my Valentine." I added: "and a consultant with _____."

Another card read: "You're at the top of my list Valentine," I added: "...to be a _____ _____ hostess. Another card: "I'm calling on you to be my Valentine," I added: "and a _____ (demonstrator/etc.). Finally, the last card read: "Can't wait to wish you a Happy Valentine's Day," I added: "and to tell you more about _____" These are just a few of thousands of kids cards out there. Mail to people who you want to invite to be your next recruit/hostess/customer. Buy extras...you can use these year round for a real *TWIST*.

Another idea is to purchase bags of conversation hearts. Invite each person to have some. (I provide small cupcake papers for them to put the hearts in; if you have something in your product line that's applicable, use it.) After everyone has their hearts, do some commercials with some of the sayings: "**Fax Me**" "You can fax an order to me 24 hours-a-day, seven days-a-week" "**Love**" (any form of the word): "I love what I do...Do you love what you do?" "**Say Yes**" to being a hostess "**E Mail**" You're welcome to join my free E-mail list. Do the *TWIST* on other sayings that you find.

Finally, let the guests take conversation hearts as mentioned above. This time, give points for each color. I always give the most points for GREEN... "Green is my favorite color because it means I'm growing personally, professionally, and financially... (share details of how your company has benefited you)." Buy extra bags of these hearts as you can use this idea all year.

Hearts to Your Business

Since sending each of you a box of candy and bouquet of flowers would be a bit difficult, I'm sending you two business ideas—a movie and cards.

I'm happy to say that I'm spending Valentine's Day with my Sweetie–we just celebrated our 25th anniversary (of our first date, and we were engaged one month later and married in June that same year!). We celebrated by watching one of our favorite movies: *Chocolat*. Every person who owns a business must see this show. When watching it, view it with the *TWIST*. Here's a preview:

A lady comes to a town and opens up a business—a chocolate shoppe! She has no family or friends in this town, and she's a single mom. She doesn't have an easy job. Her store is a real mess! But with hard work she soon has her place gleaming. However, the people in the town are not happy that she has opened this business, supposedly because it is during Lent. A few do support her efforts and her customers become her friends.

When watching this, notice she places the customer first and focuses on their wants and favorites. She has a bumpy road to travel in this city, and in fact, feels she should close shop and move on...I don't want to give any more details away. The movie is delightful and contains lessons we can all learn from as we serve our customers and ultimately create many Sweet Successes in our businesses.

I hope you all get lots of Valentine cards today (of course, you also want to give a lot away). The cards that will add more hearts to your business are business cards from other people. I am a collector of business cards. They are more valuable to me than rare collectible cards (i.e. baseball, etc.). A great way to collect these is at home presentations. Rather than doing typical "door prize drawings" with the "same old, same old" questions, simply ask everyone to enter their business card in your drawing. Be prepared with blank cards so those who do not have their own can design their own card...just like they can design their own business with your company. Before submitting the cards, ask them to code the card with one of three letters: B if she wants to Buy more of the product, G if she wants to get Gifts, or S if she wants you to Share your business plan with you by Selling your product. When talking about the S, I tell them to put a line vertically down the middle to remind them by saying Yes to the S they'll generate $.

When you have a chance to look at the cards, you'll get a feel for how the person wants to be serviced. You'll also know where she works and what she does at work; whether her company provides her with business cards; or if she's not employed at all.

Once a month, I suggest doing one drawing with all the cards you've collected. The winner gets lunch with you! What a great way to get to know customers, hosts, and new consultants. They'll always remember you for the *TWIST* you did.

Chapter Three: The Ideas of March

Happy St. Paddy's Week

I had the wonderful privilege of speaking to some wonderful Petra consultants this past weekend. I gave them a fun idea that I wanted to pass on to you, which will be great for this week: I DREAM OF GREENIE: At all your shows/parties/demos, encourage hostesses to ask guests to wear as much GREEN as possible. When guests arrive, give a reward to those with the most/least green. Then recognize those with the "weirdest" green: green makeup, nail polish, shoes (whatever you think best). Show as many products as possible with the color green, or that you can use the color green with.

Here's the part that will grow your business. Ask the group if they had their own "Genie" what are three wishes they would ask for? Have them write these down on their order form or door prize slip (something that you'll end up keeping). Let some share their wishes (this is finding out the "why" they might want to join your team and/or schedule a demonstration with you). Let them know that you are their "greenie genie" and can show them how to:

- Add more green stuff (money) to their life
- Get a new green car
- Put new green carpet in their home
- Spend more time on the golf greens
- Have more time being a real-life gardener and raising their family
- Be a 'green thumb' gardener
- See that the grass can be greener on your team's side.

Green stands for GROW and GO... Be a greenie genie that someone is dreaming of today!

March 2001: Learner of the Day

A couple of weeks ago, I walked into the lobby of the Spring Hill Suites by Marriott in Hershey, PA. As I walked in, I immediately saw a sign at the desk that said, "Welcome to our Guest of the Day...Christie Northrup." WOW...my name in "lights!" For being chosen Guest of the Day, I was able to have the breakfast of my choice delivered to my room (breakfast is complimentary in the lobby) and when I got to my room, I found a cute basket (I don't think they bought it from any of my direct sales friends, though!) filled with Hershey kisses...along with a congratulations note! Does this cost the hotel anything? Not much...the price of a few chocolate kisses. But was I impressed? You bettcha! Have I told other people about this hotel...you know I have!

As the Lemon Aid Lady, I've done a *TWIST* on the Guest of the Day at my Learning Adventures. Now, at each class, I choose a Learner of the Day. How can you implement this? For those of you with retail locations, simply display a sign like the hotel did. For those of you doing home demonstrations, use your guest list (you gotta get those...I could teach for hours on the value of these) to randomly choose someone. This is another reason to have the hostess confirm who is attending. Let her know you want to choose a "Guest of the Day"* then choose a number, count down that many on the list, and there you have it.

*The name. Come up with a fun name relative to your product: "Chef of the Day", "Candle Lover of the Day", "Collector of the Day", and so on. Simply put a sign on your display table with the person's name in "lights". Give her special attention and a very valuable (not expensive) gift. Guess who will be one of the first to be your next hostess? Our own name is the most important word to us. Highlight your customers and see your business grow.

Chapter Four: Spring Into Action

Spring is for Sponsoring

As our businesses are blossoming with the sunshine and warmth in the air, here's a fun Sponsoring Story to share:

"As you watch me do my demonstration today, you might be wondering how I ever began my career as a _____ (name of company) consultant. In fact, you may even wonder what I did before I began. We'll I've "bean" a few places along the way and am so glad I discovered _____ (your company).

"**Green Beans:** I used to work for a company/in a profession that I really liked. My paychecks were full of the green stuff I could spend. But in exchange, my family was shortchanged because the time I spent with them was as 'skinny as a bean.' I longed to be home more.

"**Lima Beans**: So, I decided to quit my job. But I went from one extreme to another. I was so glad to be home that I was lying around accomplishing nothing! I have to admit I was a 'lying around bean.'

"**Kidney Beans**: Then my kids needed me to volunteer in all their activities. My involvement with the 'kids need bean' got me moving, but I was spending a lot of time away from home, similar to my job without the green stuff! I kept looking for the perfect solution!

"**Pinto Bean:** One of my friends invited me to a home party with _____ (company name). Even though I wasn't thrilled to go, I was curious about the products. The consultant must have known what I had "bean" going through. At the end of the demonstration, she graciously invited me to an opportunity meeting and 'pinned' me down to the date and time. She even called me the next day to review the facts of the business.

"**Jelly Beans:** At this fun event, I learned how many others had "bean" where I had 'bean'. I was taught that our company is more like jelly beans: colorful, sweet and flexible. Some people joined for the money (green), others joined because they loved the product (red). Many shared how their bank accounts were now in the black because of the income. One lady shared that since joining she's seen more sunshine (yellow) in her personality! Everyone agrees that you can do whatever you want to do–you 'write' your own plan for the future (white).

"And me, the best part is I'm more balanced and happy. I finally feel like a real human 'bean'.

"Have you 'bean' where I've 'bean?' If so, let's chat! We have another fun event for all human 'beans' coming up!"

April Flowers

Do you love getting flowers delivered? Perhaps you've heard of FTD. I believe these initials stand for Florists' Tele Delivery. Are you ready for the Lemon Aid *TWIST* on FTD? Would you love BOUQUETS OF NEW BUSINESS? Read on...

FTD really stands for FOLLOW THROUGH DAY. Plan one day during this week/month to have you and/or your team focus on following through on those leads that you've "been meaning to get around to." Do nothing else during this time period but follow through. Perhaps you've planted some seeds by sending out catalogs...call these prospects and see what they want to order. Have you sent your recruiting information to someone who hasn't called you back? Guess what? They probably won't. This doesn't mean they do not have a high interest level. They have just as much going on as you do...they haven't had a chance to follow through by calling you! Do you have people in your business bank (*Deed Alphabet*, pages 18-20) who are expecting a call from you to set a date for their demonstration/show/party? Call them now! Handing out literature, mailing information, and planting seeds really is easy. The step that most people don't make is the following through...Make your Business Blossom by sending yourself and your team an FTD Day...you'll be "gladiola" that you did as you will "ROSE" to the top and have "Sweet Smelling Success!" For more information on Follow Through read pages 43-47 of the *Lemon Aid Deed Alphabet*. To order your copy, visit www.lemonaidlady.com.

Planting a Successful Business

At the Presentation$ for Profit Learning Adventures in the last couple of weeks all over the country, I've shared some fun ways to use seasonal props at your presentations. As promised, here's the script for Planting a Successful Business:

To more fully illustrate the benefits of joining your business now (in the growing season), purchase packets of some of these seeds and tell a story at your shows. On each packet of seeds, place a sticker with your name, phone, and this message, "These seeds are the beginning of a bounteous, beautiful business." Present those who appear the most interested with a packet of seeds. Invite her to plant the seeds and watch both her business and plants grow. Do you feel like you've been SQUASHED in your current position? Does your supervisor/boss SNAP at you like a DRAGON? Then, LETTUCE talk for a minute...because I've BEAN where you are and know that you MUSTARD things around. (Explain briefly how you are the one in control of your work, schedule, and income). I know it's a bit CORNy, but PEAS listen and don't TURNIP your nose or mind to what I can share with you. After all, you might find yourself lucky and green...like the BELLS OF IRELAND.

Here's another idea: "My husband (wife) is a real jewel (or gem), but I didn't MARIGOLD. With my own business I am able to CARROT about those who matter most. I can FLOWER MY SONS (and daughters) with my time and attention. Not only am I growing a happy family but also a profitable business." As you tell one or both of these stories, show the packages of seeds, OR see who can recognize the names of seeds as you tell the story. Just in case I *TWISTED* too much, the last seed packet is for SUNFLOWERS (I have all boys and they are the sunshine of my life!).

I purchased American Seeds at WalMart®, and they were ten for a dollar. Also, look for the Better Homes and Gardens "kids" brand of seeds. I found these also at WalMart. On the bottom of the Sun Flower Seeds, it says "Home-Grown Birdseed". You could use this package to say, "I can flower my sons and daughters with lots of love because I have a home-grown business." You are invited to share other *TWISTS* of this idea and your Sweet Successes and Juicy Profits from planting and harvesting this idea.

Happy April "Fulls" Month!

That's right…time to fill up the month of April. Soon you might be hearing the following excuses or reasons for not booking or selling:

• In May, "I'm planning Graduations"
• The June reason is "I'm hosting a bridal shower/planning a wedding."
• July's theme, "We're going on vacation."
• August you'll hear school bells and "We're too busy getting the kids in school."
• September's woe could be, "I need to take a rest from my busy summer!"
• October and November and December, "I'm too busy planning the holidays."

Believe it or not, these aren't replies from customers and this is not an April Fool's joke. These quotations come from the mouths of Consultants/Representatives as to reasons they are not booking and selling.

Get over those excuses, do a *TWIST* with your reasons. April is the best month of the year to have a more than FULL calendar so you can draw from a large base of new customers who will convert to your future hostesses and consultants. You might have plans for weddings, vacations, and other events—the beauty of this business is you can trade work now for those plans. Decide now to make up in time and volume for your upcoming activities. You won't feel guilty for enjoying the benefits of the business.

Eventually, the sentences above could be spoken by potential hosts and recruits. Build up your Business Bank now and keep it FULL all year long so their reasons won't be your excuses for not booking and selling–you don't want to be the FOOL.

Every season has its reason for people to say no to buying, booking, or selling. Before your calendar (and even those of your prospects) becomes to full, fill up April! You're a fool not to!

Chapter Five: Easter and Mother's Day

Grateful Plateful

When someone accepts your invitation to do business with you, put them on your calendar as a hostess or register them as a new recruit, and then... add them to your GRATEFUL PLATEFUL. This simply means to immediately send them a Thank You note. Don't wait until their show is held. Thank them NOW for scheduling business with you. Send another note after the show is held. Here's an idea:

Dear Jane:

April 28th is going to be a great day...the date of your _____ show/party/workshop/demo. Thank you for inviting me to your home to teach your friends about how _____ can help them _____ (i.e. how stamps can help them awaken their creativity, how microwave cooking can save them time, how baskets and pottery can help them decorate and organize, fit the benefit to their need specific to your company) You will be so excited when your _____ (specific hostess gift) arrives at your home! I promise to do everything in my power to make this a success for you!

(Sign your name)

Note: I faithfully used the magnets from Jenny B's Booster to enclose in every note. The magnets "It's your party" and "It's your show" have a place to write the time and date of show and your name and phone. Hostesses love them. Call Jenny's office at 1-800-5JENNYB to order (very, very inexpensive) and tell her the Lemon Aid Lady referred you. Fill your Basket with Business and your Plate with Gratitude.

Egg-citing Ideas: A *TWIST* on the Easter Egg

Recently, one of the cover stories in *USA Today* mentioned that Baby Boomers' Nest Eggs are being scrambled due to the downturn in the stock market. May I offer a *TWIST* for people who are wanting to grow a Nest Egg for their retirement...invest in Your Own Business.

By working part time in your own business and netting just $100 per week, you can save $5200 a year. Times that by how many years till you "retire" (I personally believe 65 is way too young to retire, and if you love what you do, you never have to or want to retire). Now, by investing this amount, surely your nest egg will grow faster and faster. Most people think the only way to grow a retirement fund is through an employER (gee, could that stand for "emergency room—that's how some people feel about their employment?"). You are your own security. Those few hours a week will pay dividends for years to come.

What if you only net half that amount–$50 per week? That's still $2600 per year. How many people add that extra amount to their "Nest Egg" each year?

Here are a few ways you can illustrate this at a party/workshop/show/class/team meeting/opportunity meeting. Hope you "crack up" a little over the ideas:
Are you "scrambling" to save for your retirement? Is your current pay check "hard boiled"...sometimes rotten? Well, it's time to see the "Sunny Side Up" and discover how you can grow your own "Over Easy" business. As you add more "fluff and stuff" to your business by the way of customers and team members, you'll create your own delicious business Omelette...the ultimate retirement Eggstravangza!

Nestle'® has a great new candy out for the Easter Season called NESTEGGS. They come in four delicious flavors (I know this personally). Stock up on these and use them year-round as props when you present this concept. Put them in a "fill and thrill" plastic egg. Announce that your company is "hatching" new business; open the egg, and tell this story.

The Hatch: Easter Egg II
Lemon Aid Learners: Here's an EGGSTRA Idea to help you HATCH more business every month of the year!

Now that I've been to my local WalMart® and have seen one of the most fun kinds of candy on the shelf for attracting business, I can share these ideas with you:

The candy I'm talking about is the Necco® Candy Eggs. These are similar to the heart-shaped conversation hearts you buy at Valentines. But the fun *TWIST* is on the eggs are NAMES! I believe that "names are worth millions!" So, buy a bag for about a buck and see your business blossom. Here's how:

If you are a leader, send a fun spring/Easter note to your team members. Put a handful of these eggs in the envelope–enough to keep the postage at the one stamp level. I have my postmaster hand stamp the envelopes so they don't get smashed in the machines. On the note, ask each person if they know anyone with the names that are on the eggs. Once they match who they know with the names of the eggs, ask if these persons are prospects to be a customer, host, or recruit. Challenge them to call! Or, plan a special team meeting for them to invite these names to.

When you're at your home presentations, fill the plastic "fill and thrill" eggs with these name eggs. In one or two of these eggs, place a yummy solid chocolate egg with a gold foil wrapper–you'll find bags of these where you buy the name eggs. Place the plastic eggs in your products if possible (bowls, baskets, bags, etc.) As people come in, have each person choose an egg—but don't let them open it yet. When you have everyone's attention, make this announcement:

"In _____ (company name) we're hatching lots of new business and are looking for people with special names."

Now they can all open the eggs. Ask each of them to see if they know people with these names who are over the age of 18. Be prepared for everyone to compare notes with each other's eggs. They especially get a kick out of the men's names, for some reason. Once they acknowledge that they know these people, suggest that they call these folks when they get home to tell them what a great time they had at the presentation and that they were "talked about."

Your current guests can invite their "names" to come to a presentation, or you can invite them to call you to book a party or become a consultant. Will you get referrals from everyone? Of course not! But, people will be talking about you and the fun they had and you will hatch more business. I'd be bold and have them write the names of the people they know and their phone numbers on their order form. This way, they'll remember the names (since they'll eat the egg). When you help them with their order, ask if they want to call or will they allow you to call. I actually want them to make the call.

What about those with the "golden eggs?" Make a big fuss over these people. Let them know that of all the people there, they got the golden egg. Tell them to see you after to receive some golden information about a golden opportunity with your company. Will they all come running up? Of course not! But what if half of them did, and what if half of those said YES?

There are several *TWISTS* you can do with these eggs. Once they "hatch" their eggs, you can give points for different colors of eggs: 10 for pink, 20 for white, 30 for orange, 1000 for the golden egg, etc. Award and recognize the highest points.

Or, see who has the most women's or men's names. Make a big deal over the people who received an egg with their own names. Have them match up the names on their eggs with other people at the demonstration who actually have the name. This helps people to get to know each other in a very fun way. Buy these bags by the bushel. Easter season is not the only time to "hatch" new business. If you do this at a show in July or October, or any of the months in between, will be you attracting new customers? Of course, because you did the *TWIST*…you are different…you are the BEST!

Man the Party for Mother's Day

Here's a *TWIST*...a message from Mr. Lemon Aid, Bob Northrup:

As Mother's Day approaches, men folk seek–often at the very last minute–the ideal act of love and devotion for the mother of their children. For some, it's cooking a special meal. For others, it's purchasing a gift or cleaning the house and doing the laundry. Even others may take the kids away all day, so Mom gets a rest.

Well, here's an idea they might not ever think of—one that's specific to our direct-sales industry: Have them do a party for you! That's right: have them plan, demo, and follow through, just as you would (but more clumsily). Your husband (or adult children) could host and demonstrate a party with their friends/family business associates and give you the sales and profits. If it's planned and held soon, the party could be focused around the guests buying gifts for the mothers in their lives! What a nice gift!

When Christie was out holding parties, she'd sometimes double book evenings when her party bank was overflowing, with the intent that someone in her unit would take the extra party and run with it. There were also times when she was ill and couldn't do a party. And still others when she was having babies. And she couldn't always find someone on her sales team to take on the parties. So I did…

That's right. After all, we used the products in our home and I had watched her do dozens of parties, right? I'd helped her countless times to prepare her weekly order (in the days before the Internet!), and made deliveries when she couldn't. So, why not?!

The parties were FUN. And the aspect of the "poor, helpless male" demonstrating product appealed to women's sympathy—they ordered more! I also did couples parities, where the husbands got an inside view to the direct-sales industry.

These experiences helped me to better understand what Christie was doing – the challenges, the rewards, and the great relationships she was establishing with here-to-fore total strangers. Doing parties for her was one of the reasons why I left the corporate world to work with my wife—the freedom of a direct-sales career beats the nine-to-five grind for me!

The downside? Well, I ended up doing parties in some pretty rough neighborhoods, where Christie was uncomfortable going (and yet had great parties!).

So, make the request of your husband or adult children. You'll have great sales, your customers will appreciate your man's (or children's) thoughtfulness, and in the end you'll all have a great laugh together.

And that's what's kept Christie and me going for nearly 26 years…

Chapter Six: Sweet Summer Successes

Who is Thirsty to be Your Host this Summer?

Every season has its reason for people to say "no" to buying, booking and selling. As the summer heat increases, these reasons/excuses heat up as well. So, how do you keep a full party schedule to have a sizzlin' summer of sales? Eliminate Excuses/Reasons before you Encounter them. How do you do this? With a *TWIST* on a drawing slip. An outdated (I believe) sales tactic is "overcome the objection." My Lemon Aid philosophy is to discover a person's need and follow their lead–and all succeed! (how poetic!).

To discover this need, I do a *TWIST* on the traditional door prize slip. (Note: to get the full scope of this message, refer to pages 80-84 of *Presentations for Profit$* where I teach a *TWIST* on the slip–in fact, print out this message and insert it inside your copy of the book for future reference.) Drawing slips are not only to recognize and reward guests at presentations–although that's what most people think. I use drawing slips to draw guests into the presentation and into my circle of warmth, friendship, and relationship.

So, to discover a guest's need, I suggest creating a drawing slip** specific to the season, in this case the summer. So my slip will have the guest's name (no other personal info on here!) and I ask her to circle all the summer activities she'll be participating in. Here are some examples:

• Swinging a golf club
• Shopping at the mall
• Babysitting children
• Laying on the beach
• Attending a wedding
• Going to a class reunion
• Relaxing by my own pool
• Remodeling my house
• Cooking on the grill
• Vacationing to _____ (they fill in the destination)

I like to give recognition or reward to the person with the most circles and the person with the least. This gives me an indication of their busy-ness as it can relate to my business. Those with the most circles are pretty busy and I'll adapt my service accordingly. Remember, some of the best hosts are the busiest people! Just because she has a lot of items circled, doesn't mean she's going to say "no."

As you're helping Joan with her order, you see she's marked "Attending a class reunion." This not only gives you topic for conversation, but if your product has anything to do with clothes, skin care/makeup, or dietary supplements, she's more open to your suggestions to host a presentation that has a direct relationship to a pertinent event in her life.

If a person has marked "relaxing my by own pool," suggest a pool party with your products! Attendance will likely be high! If she's going to be "Remodeling my home" and you sell home décor, that's a natural opening for a party invitation to show off her results. What if "Attending a wedding" is marked? Offer your products as a gift giving service and show her how she can get gifts she gives for free! Sure helps out on the gift-giving budget that seems to shrink in the seasons of wedding, showers, graduations, Mothers/Fathers Days!

Watch the expressions and listen for the replies as people read the slip. If someone says, "What a dream to be lying on the beach; I'm going to be attached to my office computer all summer long!" She might be very open to your business plan—especially if your company is offering an incentive to a beach destination!

Are you doing the *TWIST*? Remember I said each season has its reason for people to say "no". Why not do the *TWIST* and adapt this to other seasons? Soon, your business will be overflowing with gallons and gallons of Sweet Successes and Juicy Profits all year long !

**This drawing slip is already created in the FREE BONUS BOOKLET that accompanies the *Sweet Summer Successes* CDs.

Which Recruits would Choose You?

Here's another fun way to attract MORE RECRUITS this summer. Which recruit would CHEWS you? Purchase multi-packs of the chewing gums mentioned in this presentation. Put the sticks of gum in your baskets/bowls (whatever product you sell). As guests arrive, they each take a stick of gum. They can chew the gum, but have them save the wrapper.

Have guests listen closely and when you hold up the kind of gum they have, they yell out the name of the gum. "Is there anyone here who would like more CAREFREE time this summer, and at the same time, create some JUICYfruit PROFITS? If you want these EXTRAs, talk to me tonight. I'll show you how to DOUBLEmint your fun and $$ this summer. The best part is you get bursts of encouragement (MINTABURST) from me, my leader, and the company. And when you TRY the plan I have the only DENT you'll see is the one coming out of your checkbook (TRIDENT)." For those who seem the most intrigued, give them their own pack of customized gum (a stick of each flavor to remind them of what you just taught). And then, FOLLOW THROUGH.

Fairs (Expos & Shows) to Remember

Summer is a busy time for you to participate as a vendor at county fairs, home show expos, and other types of shows. Here are my Eight Great Tips for creating A Fair to Remember all year long: For more details and many, many other fair tips, (including some fun cards/handouts in the FREE Bonus Booklet,) listen to and apply the ideas from the Lemon Aid CDs: *Sweet Summer Successes*. Approximately 50 minutes of the CDs, and several pages of the booklet, focus on fairs.

1. Be choosy when choosing a fair. Just because you're getting a good deal on a booth, doesn't mean you should participate. The biggest questions I ask the organizer is "How much advertising are you doing? What mediums are you advertising in?" "Will my company be listed in the advertising?" I've had many disappointed clients who, after spending just $50.00 for an all day fair, didn't even see 20 people visit the booth. Small ads in the classified section of the newspaper don't count! You want an event that everyone in the city, or at least your target audience, is aware of!

2. Can you choose your booth space? The front is normally a nice place to be, and those spaces get snatched up quickly. If I can't have the front, I'd choose a place near the restrooms or food courts. Most people visit either of these places at some point during their visit. Corner booths are nice because you get extra room and can have more of an "open" booth. Sometimes you pay a premium price for the corner. It could be worth it.

3. Know your neighbors. If you sell candles, you don't want to be right next to another candle company. Know your Booth Number in advance so you can invite prospects and customers to visit (see tip #7) If you participate in a fair year after year, some organizers give you booth preference as you establish your relationship with him/her.

4. Pay for your booth in a timely manner! If the organizer has to hound you for payment, chances are, you'll be crossed off the list. Never give a bad check—your reputation will be tarnished, and so will your company's! Remember, you're telling people they can make money with your opportunity. Don't be a bad example of a great opportunity! Your customers pay you in advance; you need to be a good customer/vendor as well. Be aware of any other rules you must abide by and abide by them.

5. Have an "open" booth whenever possible. This means not having any kind of a barrier between you and your visitors, like tables. Sometimes tables are the only available option. In this case, stand to the side of the table, not behind or in front of it. My suggestion is a "U" or "L" shape set up that says "Welcome to my Store!"

6. Don't sit down on the job. Even if people are not parading through, be on your feet (wear comfy shoes!). The chairs in your booth can be used for your customers to take a load off their feet! Your standing up conveys to guests that you are ready to serve them and anxious to be of help. A couple other "don'ts": no food in the booth (unless that's your product) and don't bring your children or infants to your booth. It's just not fair to any parties involved.

7. High Touch is better than High Tech. Computers are helpful to add prospects' data after the show. If you spend all your time clicking on keys you won't connect with potential customers. Input data on the computer, if you use this mode, when you're at your desk, not your demonstration.

8. Invite current customers–especially those you haven't heard from or seen for a while– to the event. Fairs are not just to find new contacts, but also to renew business relationships. If the fair charges a fare, obtain some complimentary tickets from the show organizer if available, and send to these "golden" contacts. They'll be happy to hear from you! Send out invitations to people you haven't met yet who live near the venue.

9. Do a *TWIST* on the drawing slips you use. Remember my last message with my philosophy that drawing slips are not only for giving gifts. They're for drawing prospects into your circle of customers. Think back to when you've attended a fair as a visitor, not a vendor. You are overwhelmed by all the vendors. As you go to the booths, notice the drawing slips they hand you. Most are asking for a decision: Do you want to book a Show? Do you want to join my team? Do you want information on fundraisers or bridal showers? Etc., etc. Here's my *TWIST*: I simply want to take their temperature. I want to know how much they know about my company. So I ask them to check one box*:

A. I've LOVE _____ (company name) and have been a hostess.
B. I use _____ all the time and have attended parties
C. I've heard about _____ but don't own any
D. I haven't heard about _____ and would like to know more
E. I have no interest in _____ , I just wanted to enter the drawing.

After the fair, I divide the slips into five piles according to which box checked. All "A" go in a pile, "B" in the next, etc. Who are the first group of people I call? The As ! I find out if they are working with a consultant and are happy with the service. If so, I encourage them to call him/her. The Bs love the product and when I call I offer my services/opportunities. Likewise, I call the Cs and Ds to establish their wants/needs. I do call the Es, but they are last on the list. I call just to see if they've changed their mind and want my services. I suggest doing 2-3 drawings according to their "group." The Es are always in a drawing of their own—the winner gets a candy bar…or something similar!

This slip works very well when you are very busy at your booth. Obviously, if someone says, "I want to buy/book, be prepared to move them forward. More info on that is in the CDs.

*The Bonus Booklet has a template already made up for this type of drawing slip!

What to give away? My philosophy is something very valuable and inexpensive...your products would be the best choice in this case. In the *Sweet Summer Successes* CD, I refer to other items that can be awarded at a fair, for instance when a class is booked on site. If you want a *TWIST* on gifts to give to hosts and guests in addition to your products, we have a great resource for you: www.homeshowdepot.com.

Business Family Reunion!

Are you planning on attending a family reunion this summer? I love reunions because you get to reunite with family all over the country in one central location at a specified time. Everyone catches up on what's happened the last year. Sometimes, families don specially-made T-shirts. And, the food is always a hit! I like to not only sample everyone's dishes but also to get the recipe to take back home with me to use in my own kitchen. And whenever I do, I think of the person who shared with me.

Along with your family reunion, I hope you'll be attending your business family reunion: Your Company's Convention. Most are held June-August.

I have no "scientific proof" that those who attend annual company events excel in their businesses and have greater longevity than those who stay home. Yet, my experience tells me it is true. Here are other facts that I know from personal experience regarding company conventions:

They are worth every penny you invest, every mile you travel, and every minute you participate. If you use budgeting in your business with two separate business accounts, you'll have the funds you need to attend. Pretend attending convention is not an option if you want to continue as a consultant–those who attend stay more active.

Companies love to treat you at conventions. This is the one time of year you can be recognized and spoiled. Enjoy the pampering and recognition! And show your gratitude by your attitude and activity. By the way, sometimes what you'll hear isn't what you want to hear (changes in programs, products, compensations). Those who keep an open mind and give the new concept a chance come out champs!

Book NOW; don't wait to contact people after convention with new catalogs. To 90% of the population, your current catalog is NEW! Contact people now to take advantage of what you're offering right now. If you tell them a new catalog is out in August, they'll wait till then and you'll be waiting for more bookings and profits–that can lead to a dry summer and disappointed customers who might not get in the new catalog what they could have in the old! For those regulars who only hold parties with you at the beginning of a new catalog season, get them in your book before you leave.

Keep working on challenges to the last minute! Have you already given up on some recognition and yet the recognition time is still running? Keep working! One of the sentences I hear over and over and over at conventions is "Next year that will be me on stage!" Guess what? Next year is here! Don't whine…work…if you want something bad enough you can do it! You can make challenges and you can make excuses, but you can't make both!

Most companies open conventions to the entire sales force. What if it were only for the top 10% and you were in the top 20 or 30%. You'd be mad! So get mad and get going. Seating is usually limited to the most interested people in the business…are you one of those? People who are the most interested in their business have the most people interested in their business. These are they who attend conventions!

I am passionate about reuniting with other consultants and corporate workers this one time of year. Sometimes you dress in similar colors or wear company T-shirts to show loyalty. You always learn what's new and who has been doing what during the past year. And while the food you eat is usually yummy, the real great part of convention is taking home the business recipes shared with fellow consultants–some of whom you've never met before! In all my travels and hundreds and hundreds of conversations, I hear time and time again that businesses were transformed because of a convention–what a powerful event! Once a year…ya gotta be there! Plan and prepare now…

S'Mores Week
Current Customers
This week you can "stick to" customers who have purchased from you in the past. Simply pick up the phone and say: Julie (customer's name)! _____ (your name), calling from _____ (your company). We're celebrating s'more week and want to know if you need s'more _____ (candles, cleanser, clothes, containers….whatever your product is)." This is an easy door opener to give her information about what's new.

At Parties
On your display table, take a package of graham crackers or graham cereal, bag of marshmallows, and a chocolate candy bar. Even if your product has nothing to do with food, use this idea! Don't say anything about why you have these items on the table. You can even put a couple of ribbons around the items to attract more attention. Eventually, the most curious person will ask you "What are the graham crackers, marshmallows, and chocolate bar for?" And you reply, "This is to remind me to ask if anyone here is looking for s'more time with kids this summer, s'more money to go on vacation, s'more _____ (name of your products), etc. If you do, I have the recipe–join my company!"

You can offer one or all of the ingredients for the s'mores to the first three people who book a party from you. If you represent a company with food-related products, do a s'more party. You can make s'more brownies very easily. The last few minutes of baking, sprinkle the brownies with marshmellow and chocolate pieces...yummy, gooey...they'll all want s'more!

For your team
At you team meeting, have the same ingredients on hand. Explain that Consultants represent the marshmallows because they are the most important ingredient in sticking to customers (the graham crackers) with tasty service (chocolate bars). You can make a s'more in the microwave very quickly; about 15 seconds. After it comes out of the microwave, ask the team if anyone would love the yummy treat. Most will say yes. Then remind the team that they have the recipe to teach customers how to _____ (stamp, cook, organize, dress, etc) and people are waiting to taste their service. Challenge them to use the first two ideas at and away from their parties.

An Idea Worth Copying

One consultant told how she obtained two new bookings. She sent a friend to the store to make copies of a flyer. Fortunately for her, the friend left the original in the copy machine. The next person who went to make a copy saw her flyer and called to book at party! So, here was a "sour situation" which turned into a lot of Sweet Successes! If you don't want to give up your original, put one of the copies in its place, or leave one in the tray! And, always ask the owner of the copy shop if you can post one of the flyers. After all, you're patronizing her business, so let her help you promote yours. Businesses where copy machines are located are great places to locate leads. You must follow the first Lemon Aid Law for Locating Leads: Look, Listen, and Learn. Three times in the past two weeks while having copies made, I observed what other patrons were copying and began a conversation that introduced me to more leads who became customers! These "casual conversations" can be converted into "committed customers."

The key is to ASK the person about themselves and their interests. For example, as I was looking and listening, I had the feeling the woman ahead of me in the copy machine line at Office Max had her own business because of the dialog between her and the employee. So I inquired... "Do you have your own business?" She is a Creative Memories® consultant who I showed the *Lemon Aid Lead* book to and invited to attend my next seminar! So, as you're out making copies of your flyers, don't focus on what you're doing, but look, listen, and learn why others are at the same place. And, while we're on the subject of flyers, carry a lot of them in your purse along with a stapler, thumb tacks, and tape. Whenever you park your car, put flyers on the cars on both sides of yours. And, refer to the section in the *Lemon Aid Lead Alphabet* about Business Card flyers (page 11).

Convention Kits

With summer comes the annual company convention (some call it Jubilee, others call it Seminar. We'll just call it Convention for convention's sake!). Read on about what you need to take to your conventions...now and in the future. It's always nice to have a check off list of the most important things to take to a convention with you. Sometimes you don't think about something till you're there. I created this list from years of attending conventions...

Business cards to give other reps you'll meet so you can begin corresponding with them (much easier than writing down names/addresses/phone)

A sweater for the air conditioning in the meetings; it's difficult to learn when your brain, arms, and legs are frozen!

Very comfortable shoes (conventions are a BAD time to be breaking in new shoes...a lesson I had to learn!)

Aspirin or other headache reliever...for all the excitement. Sometimes your head just can't stand all that fun! (My good friend, Ruthie, knows I always packed this!)

A camera! Must capture as many moments as you can. If you're asked to not take pictures during a performance (it can sometimes can blind the performers), please be courteous. Be sure to get your whole group in pictures. Enlist the help of passersby to take the picture, then return the favor...you'll meet more new friends this way!

Stamps for postcards and pre-printed labels for your upcoming hostesses and your team for their postcards. Get the cards ASAP and mail them.

Dollar bills to use as tips for hotel maids (a dollar a pillow), hotel employees who assist with your luggage, restaurants servers (be generous and reward good service), airport employees at curb check in, etc. When you give them a tip, leave them with the best tip, your fun business card or catalog (get their names, too!)

Company literature/brochures to leave in the plane for the next passenger's enjoyment and to give to your seatmates (if they're not your traveling companions)

Use your **convention notebooks** for autographs for your new friends and those you travel with. Makes a great "unbuyable" rememberance (like your high school yearbook)

The most important thing: Your little **Fat Book**...this has nothing to do with the weight of the book. This is a small notebook, maybe 3 x 4 inches, spiral bound. Small enough to keep in a purse, but large enough to write on. As you listen to speakers and other attendees, you'll hear great suggestions; do your own *TWIST* on how you can apply them, write these inspirations down as they come to your mind. To me, this creative thinking is the MOST VALUABLE thing I get from a seminar/convention. I keep this separate from my meeting notes so they stand out and I know they are my own innovations. When I write them down, I use them (INK IT, DON'T JUST THINK IT!).

A tape recorder for after to record all the fun and the plans you've made. Your mind is so full; go back to the hotel and record your feelings. Ask for input from your roommates. So many great things come from the "after meeting" meetings. Keep the tape player rolling. This is a wonderful tape to play in your car on the way to shows...it's like "canning" a bit of the convention.

A smile and happy attitude, in spite of what changes might be announced. Changes, however exciting they are, can sometimes upset rather than inspire. Your company is in business for you...they are continually making improvements for you to build your business. Keep an open mind and an open heart.

Hands ready to clap for all accomplishments. Sometimes we're the cheerleaders, and sometimes we're the people being cheered *for*. Always be grateful for where you are and congratulate others for what they've done.

When you get to your convention, **divide and meet** others. Don't worry about sitting next to your friends and saving places; go out and meet new frinds. The entire convention might be video- or audio-taped, but nother compares to meeting new peole and forming freindships. This is what makes conventions memorable.

Chapter Seven: Summer Vacation

What I Did with My Business this Summer...

Do you remember writing essays in school about "What I did during my Summer Vacation?" Sometimes I would agonize thinking that what I did wasn't as cool as what everyone else did, and sometimes my summers were pretty normal...no exotic trips, etc. And, when I had to think in reverse, I had a difficult time remembering what I had done.

So, here we sit on the brink of our Summer Vacations. There are 97 days between Memorial Day and Labor Day, or in other words 14 weeks. What will you be able to say you did this summer for your business? Since you are all adult business owners, my suggestion is to write down what you're going to do now–in May– and then map it out as if you were taking a trip. Each week could be a different "destination" or mile marker about where you want to be. Give yourself souvenirs about where you've been, and send a post card to yourself acknowledging your accomplishments. And remember, every well-traveled road is under construction at one time or another. You might hit some bumps and may have to take some detours–which is wonderful because you'll get to see some new scenery.

One of the bumps is that people are busy and absent during the fun summer months. Don't fret, do the *TWIST*. In *The Lemon Aid Deed Alphabet: The Deeds you Need to Convert your Leads to Committed Customers,* on page 113, I give a fun way of keeping in touch with your customers during the summer months by having them send you a post card from their vacation destination. Promote this in your place of business and at your home demonstrations. Hand out pre-addressed labels with your name and address. After you receive their post cards, call them to thank them and talk about their vacation. This will be an easy way to open the door for marketing opportunities. Encourage customers to do this by offering to send them a postcard with a bonus offer for your products after you receive their card (just say they'll receive a surprise from you in the mail). Then, at the end of summer, invite all those who participated to a special event where you can show your holiday items (only invite those who participated...keep this exclusive). At the event, use the post cards for recognitions and drawing for new products. This is another fun way to keep in touch by servicing and involving your customers.

What are You Doing with Your Business?

Many of you have asked why you didn't see many–or any–cities that I was going to be speaking in during the past year. Thanks for your concern. Now, if you've known me for a while, you know I have done a lot of traveling in the past three years to come to as many cities as possible.

About a year ago, I examined what I was doing. I was out telling you how to build your businesses and work from home. However, I was hardly at home. And our business was growing so much that I moved my office out of my home and hired some employees to help out. *I had a real wake up call when I realized I wasn't living what I was teaching.* Many people commented that I was lucky my kids were older so I was able to travel. This is true, but kids still like to have mom around–and mom likes to be with the kids! More importantly, I was missing my husband. We've had a great marriage for many years (25 this June!), and I wanted to be sure it continued to be great. Quick phone calls to each other while on the road and passing each other in airports (he also had a heavy travel schedule) were just not the way to keep a family close. So, I cut way back on my travel schedule–only doing company- specific events that I could get to and from in a day or two–and I moved my office back home.

Through the years, many of you have expressed concern about the very challenges I've just described. How do we keep our business and family growing? After all, isn't that why most of us have chosen this industry? For 22 years, since my oldest son was a year old and through two additional pregnancies and several moves, I've encountered this. And believe me, the challenge remains if your child is one, 11, or 21. And, for the most part, I've been very pleased with our business and family progress. There are also things I'd change.

This past spring our youngest turned 18 while our oldest announced that he and his wife were expecting our first grandchild in late November. That's when my husband and I began to do the Lemon Aid *TWIST*. We realized that as we become grandparents, we will have come full circle. Our children have been raised with the best of both worlds: a stay-at-home mom who runs a successful business. And now a new generation begins.

You might say we're in the Autumn of our lives. We are now in a position to share our passion, plans, and purpose for having a direct sales business at home with more of you. We–both of us–are ready to travel *together* to bring two new Lemon Aid Learning Adventures to you. (My husband, Bob, has worked with me at various levels throughout the years. I'm sure you and your spouse will enjoy the perspective he brings to the classes.)

Between now and the end of November, we will be visiting nearly 60 cities–see bottom of this message – (we'll be home in December to be with the new grandbaby!) and will add more cities the first quarter of next year. Our goal is to get to every area of the country in the next nine months.

So, which slice of life are you in? Spring, Summer, Fall, or Winter? How can you take advantage of the stage your family is in?

Take Your Business to the Beach

You can do this to attract recruits a couple of different ways. 1. Use a couple of these props at your demonstrations using the wording I'm supplying 2. Schedule a Business Opportunity Meeting and invite the prospects to bring a beach towel and join you at a beach party. Purchase some of these props at a discount or dollar store:

SAND CASTLE TOYS: How many of you work in a castle, for royalty? I do...because your home is your castle, I come to your home to demonstrate _____ (your product) and I treat you like royalty. In addition, every day, I work at my own castle–my home! My company treats me like royalty because (share benefits of your company and specific, personal examples)

BUCKET AND SHOVEL: Just like all the sand on the beach, millions of people are waiting to be serviced by _____ (your company). I can't do it all myself, but I can teach you how to create BUCKETS OF BUSINESS by shoveling more people, profits, and fun into your life.

INFLATABLE SWIM RING: You see, _____ (your company) can really PRESERVE your life this summer because _____ (give specific reasons why; use the "Life Saver Idea" from the archives file of this list for more detailed info on using this idea). NOTE: Be sure you are "inflated" not "deflated" about your business, you can't PRESERVE another's life, if you're not CONVINCED you have the best to offer!

PLASTIC TOY BOAT: When you join _____ you will be able to Sail into September without worrying about paying for school clothes, tuition, and other expenses that cause "waves" in your budget. A *TWIST* for those of you who have "cruised" compliments of your company or whose companies are offering upcoming cruises as an incentive: "How many of you have CRUISED at no cost? _____ has allowed me to cruise at _____ _____ (places you've gone). Jump on the boat now, so you can join us at our next destination of _____.

BEACH BALL: As a consultant with _____ customers will BOUNCE BACK to you all the time because we have _____ (great hostess program, monthly specials, new products, etc.

FLIP FLOP SANDALS: Some of you might be cautious about committing because you're not sure if this will work for you. Remember, "I have been in your shoes; I know the reservations you might have. I'm here to teach you and walk beside you as you build your business."

BEACH TOWEL: "You'll notice this isn't a regular bath towel...it's BIG for the BEACH. Just as _____ isn't a regular business, it's BIG...you will want to stay wrapped up in it!"

SUNGLASSES: Your future is so BRIGHT with _____, you'll really be needing these.

POPSICLE: (This is the refreshment I recommend handing out at the Business Opportunity Meeting as people come in–use the kind that come in the plastic long wrappers you buy in huge boxes and they last a day or two if your home is like mine!) "Just like this frozen treat will melt if you don't eat it, this opportunity will melt before your eyes if you don't join our beach soon!" "You can sit on the beach and watch everyone else swimming, surfing, and having fun. Or you can DIVE in and join us today...you won't know if this is what you want to do till you get in and get wet."

Business Beach Party–Opportunity Meeting

Here's a *TWIST* for a fun business opportunity meeting. We know that people will be getting back from vacations. We know that they might have their credit cards maxed out. They might be spending a little more time around the kids–meaning they need a little break without leaving the kids ten hours a day. Kids are going to need school clothes and a lot of moms especially are going to start looking for something they can do extra besides driving the school bus, or working in the school lunchroom.

So I have a really fun idea for you; it's called taking your prospects to a business beach party.

All summer when you meet people and think, "Oh my goodness, she would be so great to have on my team; I really want to recruit her" then you'll give her an invitation that says simply, "Swim on over to hear more about" and then you fill in the name of your company. It also asks them to bring a beach towel. You can buy "pool party" invites or make your own.

If I want to tell her more about my business, and I tell her to bring a beach towel, do you think I'm going to peak her interest? Or do you think she's going to think, "Oh yeah, I'm going to hear about making more money, yadda, yadda, yadda." No, she knows it's going to be something different because you're inviting her to your business beach.

As people come in–by the way, I just do this at my house–I don't want to go be renting a big hotel room. They bring their beach towels. Have extra ones in case people forget so they won't be embarrassed. They can just sit on the floor on their beach towels. Once they're comfortable and sitting down, I give each of them a Popsicle®.

Now I begin to tell them about my company and why it is so unique. I present this by using starfish. You can buy these by the dozens at novelty stores if you don't live by the beach. I have these starfish scattered around my living room, or a family room, wherever you're at. And I pick up one of the starfish and I say, "You know, just like this starfish has five different points to it, I'm going to tell you about five things that make (fill in your company's name) so unique, so different from any other company.

Now, look at your business and think, "What sets my company apart from other companies? Why did I choose my company? Is it because we have the very, very best kitchen tools? Do we manufacture our own products so they can't be purchased anywhere else? Do I get paid the minute I make a sale? Does my company offer a car or a home mortgage incentive program? Each company has its individual uniqueness. What is it that sets your company apart?

Let me tell you what not to say. Don't say, "Oh, because you can set your own hours, and you can make your own money," because guess what? You can do that working at the gas station now because companies are letting people use flex-time all over the place, and they'll let you work as many hours as you want. So those are a given in direct selling. Discover the difference that your company offers.

Now, as you're presenting keep the information to only ten to 15 minutes–you don't need to go into great depth. For those people who are real interested, you can dive in with them later.

Next, I say, "You know, there are just a few of you who are here today, and I'm so glad that you're here. And now I've told you about the five points that make our business so spectacular, but I want to share a story with you about starfish.

As you can see here in my living room, I've got dozens of starfish- these poor starfish–they got out of the water a little too early. And you know what happens to starfish when they're out of the water? They die.

I'm going to tell you a story about a little boy and his grandpa. They were walking down the beach together, and every few feet, grandpa would pick up a few starfish and throw them back into the ocean. After about 15 minutes, the grandson asked in a puzzled tone, "Grandpa, why are you throwing those starfish back in the water?"

Then Grandpa explained to him and he said, "Honey, you know we like to collect these little starfish–they're all over the beach–but if they're not in the water, they'll shrivel up and die. I don't want them to die, so I'm throwing them back in the water."

The little boy said, "But Grandpa, there're so many of them. You're never going to be able to help all of them."

Grandpa wisely answered, "I know," as he picks up more starfish and tosses them far out in the ocean—"but I helped that one didn't I?"

This story has a lot of impact–how does it relate to your business beach party?

Well, after I tell that story in my business opportunity beach, I've got their attention. Then I proceed: "You know, of all the people in the world, you were the only ones I could invite to come to my house today. I would love to share my business opportunity with everybody, but it just wasn't possible to get everybody here. Just as the starfish that got thrown back in the water, you're the people that I could talk to today. And I hope I'm able to save your life and to save your finances, and other things in your life that you need with our business opportunity."

"And I noticed that some of you ate those Popsicles®. Weren't they just great? Wasn't that such a refreshing treat? And then I noticed that some of you haven't opened yours yet. Well, you know, if you don't take advantage of my business opportunity, it's going to melt, just like this popsicle. So I hope you all take advantage of just giving us a try." And then you can go on and explain how that works.

If you use the business beach and this story, you will catch the attention of these prospects. And if you do it with a sincere heart so that people know that you really care about them, your business beach is going to grow, and grow and grow. You're not just going to have a little strip of the beach. You are going to have miles and miles of businesses. Your team will grow, your hostesses will grow. You're going to be happier and then you're going to go into the fall selling season and the holiday selling season with gallons and gallons of Sweet Successes and Juicy Profits.

A Cure for the Business Slump

I don't eat or drink any dairy products (I have a real aversion to cheese, especially). So, taking a calcium supplement is really important so I don't slump with osteoporosis in my old age. But, sometimes I get so busy I forget! Then, I realized if I keep the bottle out on my kitchen counter, I see it often and remember to take it twice daily. When something is visual, we seem to take action. May I suggest this summer that you create a VISUAL DIMINISHING GOAL. As you decide what you will do with your summer business, pick something visual to constantly remind you of the goal and put it in your face! For example, if you want to hold three shows a week during the next 13 weeks, you will need to have held 39 (so I'd schedule at least 50). What kind of Visual Diminishing Goal could you use? I suggest something to send to every hostess.

My friend, Jenny B of the Booster–1-800-5JENNYB**, sells wonderful magnets that say "It's your Show", "It's your Party", "It's your Class". I would purchase 50 of these (they are VERY affordable) along with some Thank You Notes. As you schedule new demonstrations, write the hostess a thank you note and include a magnet...great advertising for you as your billboard will be on her fridge 24/7/365! Your goal is to GET RID of all 50 magnets. DO NOT put these in a desk drawer. They must be placed where you will SEE THEM ALL THE TIME TO REMIND YOU OF YOUR GOAL. As the magnets and thank you notes (your visual goal) diminishes, your business will GROW! Do the *TWIST* to think of other ways to use a VISUAL DIMINISHING GOAL for making phone calls, setting up opportunity appointments, sales goals, etc. E-mail me and let me know the kinds of VISUAL DIMINISHING GOALS you use and the RESULTS. This "CALLSEEUM SUPPLEMENT" will help build a strong, strong business. You won't have to worry about a business slump (a la osteoporosis)!

**When you call Jenny to order, tell her The Lemon Aid Lady recommended her.

Chapter Eight: The Fourth of July and Patriotism

Put Your Product on Parade

A much-loved summer event is a traditional hometown parade. You'll attend these often during the next three months as communities celebrate national, regional holidays and sponsor town festivals. Why not be part of the parade? Most communities welcome parade participants, particularly if the participants are members of the community or surrounding cities.

To be part of a smaller community parade, you typically don't have to have a large, float. Depending on the guidelines, you might be able to have your kids decorate their bikes and wagons and carry a banner with your name and business represented. Or, if your product is of a decorative nature, you might want to create a float on a smaller scale. As always, involve your team. Maybe you'll just be walking the parade route with a fun, wide-brimmed hat decorated with a couple of your products–anything to get attention! Even wearing a T-shirt or other logo clothing could work.

The part of the parades that people love is when participants walk along and hand out goody bags or treats. They're normally for the kids, so why not make a bag for mom and kids. Put your literature (small mini catalogs are great for this even if they're outdated–gets your name out there), business card, gift certificate, etc in inexpensive bags along with a few pieces of wrapped candy.

Many cities will have a parade to kick off their celebration days and during the festivities local businesses have booths and exhibits. If you can have a booth at the festival, put the booth number on your parade banner and/or literature. (For more ideas in being a vendor, listen to the *Sweet Summer Successes* CD and use some of the reproducible cards in the Bonus Booklet to hand out at the booth or during the parade).

The only "sour situation" with a parade is you're normally not talking to individual people as you're parading through town. You'll hand out your information without getting their names and phone numbers. So, in the goody bag, be sure to make them an offer they can't refuse when they call you to place an order or book a party.

And, even if you're not able to be in an actual city parade, be sure you're always parading your product this summer as you go about your daily activities and during your travels.

Three Cheers–and Recruits–for the Red, White and Blue!

Next week, citizens of the United States will celebrate Independence Day. Previously, patriotic symbols decked in red, white, and blue, were only found as we approached this holiday. Now, however, most stores and many direct sales companies are carrying these items as baseline products. Thus, you can use this lead idea year round.

Before your party, ask the hostess to have guests wear/bring something to the party that is red, white, and/or blue (can be all three or just one or two of the colors). Of course, this creates curiosity and many people will show up just to see why you've requested this Make sure you deck yourself in red, white, and blue as well. I found some fun plastic necklaces at the dollar store that fit the bill.

As the party progresses, do a "Fashion Show." Reward/recognize those with the most of the requested colors. Or, the person who brought the most unique items with these colors, or whatever other items you choose. I suggest giving 3 Musketeer candy bars for the prizes because the packaging shows these colors. Have a lot of fun! You can even demonstrate the patriotic products in your line or show products featuring one or more of these colors. (For more ideas and explanation on this concept, read all about Featured Attractions in *Presentations for Profit$*, pages 61-68).

After you've focused on the Red, White, and Blue throughout the party, it's time to pose a question. Ask the group: "Is there anyone here who is BLUE because your checkbook is in the RED and you don't know how to get your finances WHITE? If so, be sure to order a kit from our company–it comes complete with ME ! The average consultant nets approximately $_____ at each party. If you would shout HOORAY for that much extra cash, I'll VOTE for you to be on my team ! Remember, we're AmeriCANs, not American'ts. We have a great privilege to live the American Dream with a business of our own."

Here's something that can add to the fun. I purchased some Stars and Stripes hand clappers from Oriental Trading (www.orientaltrading.com) and then let everyone use them to clap for the Red, White, and Blue! Lastly, I told them when they voted for themselves to be a demonstrator on my team, they could keep the clappers so they can get used to all the applause they'll be receiving.

If you live in a country other than the US, use the colors of your country's flag; many use red, white, and blue. If you have some green in your home flag and your paper currency is also green, lucky you! You can mention, "If you're BLUE because your checkbook is in the RED, and you want more GREEN)... If your paper currency is BLUE, ask if you want more BLUE to get rid of the financial BLUES.

Keep in mind, we're all CANs: MexiCANs, CanadiCANs, AustrlaliCANs, BritishCANs (okay, so I really had to do the *TWIST* on a couple; please don't be offended!) We can do anything we set our mind to because we have the backing of wonderful companies and political freedoms as well.

For other lead ideas along this same line refer to the following topics in the *The Lemon Aid Lead Alphabet: Where to find Customers when you run out of Family and Friends*: Independence Day, page 60; Rewards and Recognition, page 95; Holidays, page 59.

The Power of the Party—Raise Our Business Flags Proudly

Note: While this originally was published shortly after the attack on September 11, 2001, it seems appropriate to place this message with the Fourth of July and Patriotism.

Hello Lemon Aid Learners: It's been a few weeks since my last message, and what a few weeks we've experienced! It's now been twenty-one days since one of the greatest tragedies we've known…

While some of us are more directly affected than others, we are all victims of people whose goal is to put terror and tragedy in our lives. Most Americans, indeed, many world citizens wondered, "What can I do to help?" Not everyone was able to dig through rubble, donate blood, hug survivors, or assist in other ways.

However, as home-based business entrepreneurs we can now become volunteers in a war that is raging in all our own neighborhoods…the economic downturn that has happened in the last 21 days. In the past week, we've heard of the trickle down economic effects. Literally thousands of people have or will lose their jobs. As direct sellers, there is much we can do to boost the economy of our nation while growing our businesses. It is time to *TWIST* from victim ranks to volunteer status and take action–this will show our true patriotism. We all know that our business opportunity can be the lifesaver people need in times like this…thank heavens now one else can downsize us except…US!

So, yes, we have huge pools of recruiting prospects. However, in order to keep our companies growing, millions of people and their industries provide products and services that allow us to have our own businesses. Many of these positions have been or will be eliminated, that could hurt each of us. Have you taken the time to think how many people you keep employed as a direct seller? Let's take the scenario of scheduling a home presentation.

First, you provide your hostess with literature that a printing company was contracted to print. The printer purchased ink and paper for the literature. You helped people in both those industries as well, not to mention the buildings, equipment and other supplies the printer and his/her vendors use. You or your hostess mail out the invitations. You're keeping the US Postal Service in business…but not only the employees you see at the counter and those who sort behind the scenes. Stamps must be printed–we're helping the printing industry again. Someone picks up the mail in a truck that was purchased from an automobile company–an ailing industry right now–and will need gasoline and other automotive equipment. In many cases the mail is sent on planes (if your hostess is inviting EVERYONE she knows). Someone is paid to handle the bags of mail and get it on the planes. Then private or commercial carriers…who employ thousands of people (at least until lately)…get the mail to the post office in the areas where you or your hostess are sending things. Then someone else personally delivers the mail.

Meanwhile, back at home, you're using your telephone service to connect with the hostess…and at the same time benefiting the telecommunications industry. Your hostess is using her phone and probably thinking about what kinds of refreshments she'll serve…so she goes shopping and buys cookies. Thank Heavens, those little elves will be kept busy baking if we keep them supplied with lots of hostesses! While she's at the store, she sees other things she needs and spends a minimum of fifty dollars. Each of those dollars helps support the companies whose products she just purchased, not to mention keeping the local stores in business–which employ your neighbors and friends…your future customers and recruits! When guests come to the party, they usually drive (remember, she invited people from all over). They are using gasoline and automobiles to get there, or even the local mass transit system—all of which employ people. If they didn't want to bring their children and hubby is at work or out of town, your guests might hire a teenager to watch the kids. A teenager who will keep the malls in business with the wages they receive.

Now your guests arrive and BUY YOUR PRODUCT. Who are they helping? Not just you and your hostess but also the factory that produces your product. The employees of the factory are not the only ones involved. Think of the people who work in the factories of the vendors who supply materials to your company's factory. In many cases your company uses several factories and numerous vendors…think of all the people each of these employ. Your company also has management support teams who help you market your product. These departments range from accounting to computer support to marketing to training to the building engineers who keep the facilities clean. Each of these departments uses computers, paper, office furniture, utilities, and other supplies. You are helping each of them retain their positions along with the people who work for the companies providing the services and products they consume.

Now you're excited and so is your hostess because everyone thanks you both for having the demonstration to get them out of their homes and away from the bad news TV sets. They are so thrilled to see your sunny smile, pleasant personality and feel of your selfless service as you teach them about how your product will benefit them. They have FUN! Several guests schedule more demonstrations…and the cycle multiplies.

But wait...you just earned some big bucks! Now you can go pick up the lay away you had at the mall, pay for your son's soccer registration, invest in some of your favorite stocks, take the family out for a celebration dinner, and on and on. How many people's lives will you bless by shopping, eating out, investing? But there is more: As you continue to do this you'll be a "people magnet" who will attract others to join your team, and there will be more consultants to service more hostesses who will add to the economic stability in more people's lives. Further, the more people who have more paychecks, the more they'll have purchasing power at your parties.

This keeps getting better...as you sell more of your product and share with more people, you qualify for your company's car program and/or earn promotional gifts. Can you do the "lemon link" yourself and picture who has a job because you've done yours so well?

Now the best news: you realize you've qualified for the incentive trip. Hooray! Hooray! Now, you just keep helping more and more people. Your company contracts with a travel service all run by real human beings who make all the arrangements. They purchase airline tickets, ground transportation, hotel accommodations, local entertainment and yummy food! Additionally, you take your own spending money and add to the location's tourism business. Putting more paychecks in more people's pockets. WOW!

Can you see the potential MILLIONS of people whose lives you can reach without actually touching or meeting them? Can you see the way direct selling professionals can give our nation an economic jumpstart? Remind those who suggest you get a "real job" about how you're helping jobs be a reality to millions of people. President Bush and other leaders have encouraged us to move forward in our lives while always remembering those who have and will sacrifice for our freedoms–the very freedom that allows us to have our own businesses and choose the lifestyles we want for us and our families.

It's time to raise our business flags to full staff and wave the benefits of our product and business plan. According to statistics from the Direct Selling Association (DSA), over 11 million Americans are involved in the industry. Let's say that only 1 million of us join the volunteer positions and go out and promote our business...let's say we all promise to get on the phones and call at least 50 people in the next 13 days to show our own "stars and stripes." And then in the following 50 days…that's now until Thanksgiving week (but we'll say the end of November)…all one million of us hold at least 13 parties/shows/workshop.

I tried to figure what the dollar growth to the economy would be if each demonstration averaged only $300 in sales (very average). How many dollars would that be: 13 million parties/shows/workshops x $300 equals $3.9 Billion! That's a bunch of bucks. Then, we can all say that we each contributed to helping another person provide for his/her family.

Here's one more *TWIST* on how your volunteer status can add even more. In addition to building your own business, decide to host a party of your own from another company during this same time period. Think about a hostess, customer, or friend who is a consultant for a business whose products you love. Pick up the phone, share this challenge with them (we're looking for ONE MILLION), and get in their book as well. Next, before you go to the mall, examine what you'll be purchasing. Is this item something sold by a direct sales company? Not only can you sell...you can buy through a direct selling company...which will build everyone's businesses and beyond and strengthen not only the national economy but our family's future! Time to take the "anchors of our discouraged minds away", "march over to the phone" and "fly into mild homes" of our hostesses to protect and build our personal homes and the nation's home front.

During World War II, women had to leave their home to protect the home front and work in factories to provide supplies for our troops. We so blessed to live in the United States; we can support our nation by building our home-based businesses! We've been victims, now let us join the ranks of economic volunteers and become VICTORIOUS! Make every day a V-Day!

Chapter Nine: The Dog Days of Summer

August

Can you name the first person who joined your company? What about the first to sell in your city or state? Who is the first person who sold over $50,000 in a month or year? Do you know the first person on your team to book ten shows in a week? This summer while traveling to conventions, I arrived at an airport in a city that I had never flown into. After getting my baggage, I was trying to find the recommended shuttle service to drive me into town. I went to the door I was directed to, but saw nothing. I went out to the curb, and didn't see any vehicles with the name of the company I was looking for. After asking some flight attendants who regularly take this shuttle, they told me where to go make my connections. When I finally discovered the "office in the wall" of this company and inquired about a ride, the main guy was very bothered and rude. His answers were sharp. He kept looking at his computer screen and didn't act at all interested in assisting a customer.

Quite frankly, I was appalled! This man was the first citizen of that town who I met. I was not impressed with my first impression of that city. A couple of years ago, in another city, a quiet, young man was the driver of a hotel shuttle I was on. He wasn't very talkative (and believe it or not, I am!). I began asking him questions about his job, his school, his future. He opened up a little bit. And then I told him, "You are the most important employee at your hotel." He was stunned and said, "I'm only the shuttle driver!" I then explained he was the most important because he was the first connection I had with that property, and his actions can help me feel welcome, indifferent, or anxious about the place where I was going to spend two nights. He still remained neutral; I could tell he didn't love or hate his job...it seemed to be just a job.

The next day after my Learning Adventure, his supervisor came by to see that the facilities had been satisfactory. She was curious about what I do; I explained that I had just taught a class on team leadership. She was lamenting that her staff needed some help. I shared my experience with her shuttle driver. She said, "He is really a good worker." Then I asked her, "Have you told him that?" She stopped in silence.

Now, where am I going with this *TWIST*? When marketing your product or service, in order to stand out from everyone else, you must be one of three things:

1. The first to do something
2. The best in your field
3. Different enough for people to remember you. If you've been to "Presentation$ for Profit" class, you'll know I teach how to do number three on the list...create a difference.

I've always thought that not everyone can be the first to have excelled; however, I've *TWISTED* my thinking on this. YOU CAN BE FIRST. Here are some of the categories you can be first in: First person a customer has met from your company; First person who made a guest at a show feel welcome; First person who sent a thank you note to a hostess for booking a party; First person who was on time; First person who finished on time First person who kept promises; First person who followed through; First person who offered the business plan to someone; First person who listened to a customer's complaint; First person who smiled today; First person who really cared. You never know when you'll be the first in someone else's life. Be that NUMBER ONE person today!

Bet on Your Business

August means county fairs and harness racing. And for some that means betting. Others find their gambling at other establishments, such a convenience stores…

If you live in or near a state that participated in the PowerBall® lottery, you know last week was an exciting one! Pictures on TV showed long lines–including people from neighboring, non-participating states–driving to purchase what might be their "pot of gold at the end of the rainbow." And of all those millions and millions of people, only three received a significant return–even after waiting all that time in line!

How much have you invested in this or any lottery game in the past year? This includes slot machines and other gaming devices as well–anything where you've given money in hope (and I mean hope) of getting huge sums of cash in return. (We won't include the stock market as a gamble in this discussion.) Do you know how much was paid out? And, how much was gained? In most cases, the pain of losing was greater than the gain of earning. Have you wondered why there is such a frenzy when the chances are so slim? And, yet when more of a sure thing (calling our customers to update them on what we can offer them, checking back with someone who asked to call at a later date, etc.) exists for our ultimate (and often immediate) profit and growth, we aren't willing to take action.

We're "afraid" of rejection! What do you call playing and not winning the lottery? It's rejection that we pay money for! Most states began their lotteries to add to the education funds. However, many people question if the earmarked funds ever make it to the education budget. Here's a *TWIST* and a way to insure that money you'd spend on the lottery will fund your own personal education and business growth. Next time you're at the convenience store or gas station and decide to spend a couple of bucks on a "chance," pocket that money. Do this a couple of times until you've saved $20 to $30. Then march to a bookstore or log on line to purchase food for your mind that will help you grow both personally and professionally–inspirational books, tapes, and magazines. (Jim Rohn, a great philosopher and businessman, teaches that if you feed your mind you'll never have to worry that you won't have money to feed your body!) Unlike the lottery, two things will happen. First, you won't be an instant winner. Rather, you need to digest, not simply "scratch the surface" of what you read or listen to. Second, unlike spending the money on the lottery, you'll have a permanent possession of what you spent your "extra" money on and you can go back and read/listen to it over and over. Like savoring a great meal whenever you're hungry.

Recommendations: I definitely recommend anything written by leaders/founders of any direct sales company. These include Dave Longaberger's book, *Longaberger: An American Success Story*, Doris Christopher's (Pampered Chef) *Come to the Table*, Mary Kay Ash, *You Can Have it All*. A couple wonderful books given to me so I don't know if they are still in print are *You Can Too* by Mary Crowley, founder of Home Interiors and *How to put your Wishes to Work* by Brownie Wise, the creator of the party plan system for Tupperware. If these last two aren't available at bookstores of Amazon.com, check with your friends in these companies.

Six Flags that Your Business is in Trouble

Amusement parks are fun places to visit during the summer months. And, while you're there you can even do some natural prospecting. But, don't get your business in an Amusement Park mode; you won't be amused with the results.

Six Flags that your business is in Trouble:

1. Merry Go Round Flag: You keep going around and around doing the same things, having the same sour situations–you're not very merry. Do the *TWIST* on what your are doing. Use the easy, creative ideas you learn on this list and in the Lemon Aid books and tapes.

2. Roller Coaster Flag: Your calendar is like a roller coaster. Some days it's up–and then a quick whoosh–it's down–enough to make you want to throw up! Keep consistent this summer–even if it's just one to two demonstrations each week. Consistent activity brings consistent income and growth.

3. Video Arcade Flag: You keep spending money hoping that the more you'll spend, the more you'll make. This is like dumping coins in the video arcade machines. Yes, you do need to invest in products and literature. And, once you make that investment in the business tools–use them! Don't make only the printer or the post office rich!

4. Ferris Wheel Flag: Your attitude is only fair. You go to a business meeting and get all "pumped up." Then, you feel a jerk and the wheel turns...your attitude dwindles...you pick yourself up a bit...then you see the vision again...only to be jerked some more to a less-than-fair outlook. This is the Ferris wheel flag when you know your business is in trouble. Every day read positive books, listen to positive tapes, write positive notes to yourself and others. Keep the vision and work toward the goal.

5. Bumper Car Flag: This indicates that instead of going out on the open road to find more customers, you spend a lot of time talking to other consultants on the phone or computer and talk about all the things that are going wrong in your business–from company policy to your pitiful performance. You're in a car–so to speak–and you keep bashing others–hoping that you'll come out the winner. But you won't. If you have a complaint, talk to your sponsor or to the company directly. Crashing and bashing only cause bumps and bruises–and sometimes casualties.

6. Fun House Flag. Our businesses are fun! However, the Fun House at an amusement park takes us out of reality and some times distorts what the truth is. To grow a business, you need to examine yourself in a correct mirror–not one that makes you look better or worse than you are. Track your progress at least weekly. Honestly assess your progress–and you'll see more real fun and profits!

Chapter Ten: School's In Session

Forward Eyes

Last week, my friend and her two little boys stopped by to visit. The older of the two is starting kindergarten next week. I noticed something different about him: he was wearing glasses! He was proud of his new "specs," but mom was concerned that the other kids might tease him and call him "four eyes." Interesting how she was concerned, even though now her son could see more clearly.

As we begin "Back to School; Forward in Business," what is our vision like? Are we just looking at our business a week (or should I say "a weak") at a time? Or do we have "forward eyes?" Are we concerned what others will say as we continue to correct our vision of our business? Or do we go forward without regard to others' comments and sometimes criticism?

Forward eyes have a clear vision of not just today, tomorrow, and next week but a vision of next month, next quarter, next year, five years from now and so on. Forward Eyes become clouded and smeared just like when we wear real glasses. But Forward Eyes can also clean the glasses and keep looking forward.

What do you see as the future of your business between now and the end of the year? Are you keeping that vision in clear focus every day? What will you be doing a year from now? Are your eyes focused forward on that?

People like doing business with people with Forward Eyes. Customers know you'll be around to service them; consultants know you'll be around to lead them. I'm doing some consulting work with a company that has a 100-year business plan! I know they are focused on the long term and helping people today, even though most of those people won't be around to really see the vision come to fruition.

Some of us over forty have not only Forward Eyes but "biforward vision" as well. This is another important part of vision. While we're focused forward, we need to work today. This is the close up daily, weekly work we do such as customer contacts, recruiting follow through, and so forth. Both activities forward and biforward are the prescription for healthy vision.

Before going forward in your business, check your vision. If need be, get a new prescription so you'll have Forward Eyes–and you won't care at all what others say...you'll be so focused with your own clear vision that others will want to be part of it as well!

Subjects for Booking and Selling

It's Back to School...and Forward in Business with the Lemon Aid Lady! One of the features of our popular Sweet Summer Success CDs is the list of people who are likely to be hostesses with you during the summer. Now that it's fall, here's a list of people subjects you'll want to connect with to be your next host or sales contacts (for those who do not market on a home party plan):

First of all, check your **HISTORY**—people who are already your committed customers and hostesses. See which of your customers/hostess qualifies for one of the following subjects:

MATH: This person had the highest sales of any hostess/customer. Or, the most people in attendance, or the most bookings at her demonstration. You could even add up the dollar amount of her class, each person who attended/ordered is worth $20 and each booking $50. Now ADD up the total. Call all hostess/customers over certain increments ($500/$750/$1,0000).

ENGLISH: Which of your hostesses/customers loves to gab? And which do you love to talk with? Not only are these great hostesses/customers, but also fun consultants!

HOME EC: Which of your customers/hostess are work-at-home women? Meaning, they have their own business–not just direct sales businesses? These include accountants, consultants, and graphic artists. Many times they don't have a lot of interaction with other people and having their friends over would be a nice treat.

ART: Which hostess/customer has the most decorated house, or which one(s) just remodeled and might be looking for an excuse to show it off?

CHEMISTRY: Which hostess/customer have you really clicked with? You know, the ones who have a lot in common with you? Maybe your kids attend the same school, you go to church with her, live in the same subdivision?

RECESS: Which people are the most fun and fun-loving?

FOREIGN LANGUAGE: Who is from another country/culture? Many times your product is new to them and they are great hostesses–especially if they end up sending the products to their homelands.

P.E.: Which customers/hostesses are involved in sports? Perhaps they are players or even promoters. This is the category for the soccer moms. Great leads for fund raisers !

BUSINESS: These customers/hostesses are busy with their jobs. They need a fun break!

COMPUTERS: Which customers order often from your website? Or, love to surf the Internet?

Here are the words to say: "_____ (customer name)! _____ (your name) calling with _____ (your company). Now that school is in session, I've thought about you because (you are so fun to be around, you had the highest sales so far this year–or ever, you are involved with sports, etc. etc.). Is this a good time for you to schedule a demonstration with me and _____ (your company)?
Or, "Is this a good time to see what's new with _____ (your company).
Or, "Is this a good time to get together?
If you choose five people from each category, and CALLED THEM you'll likely get five new bookings! That will put you at the Head of your Class!

Forward in Business: Physically and Fiscally Fit

School's in...are you moving forward in your business? You will physically–then financially and socially–move forward when you use this idea.

Your business will be more fit (and so will you) when you go for a walk in your neighborhood. I live in a fairly new development consisting of approximately 100 homes. I drive in and out of the neighborhood in different directions on a regular basis. I know most of the neighbors on "my end" of the street. Other than that, we just give a friendly Texas wave to everyone else.

Recently, I've been diligent at walking a couple of miles a day around my neighborhood, and I've learned some great tips for building a business. Here's my observation: When you walk rather than drive, you get a microview of your neighbors. And when you do this on a regular basis, you'll get to know information about how you can help your neighbors with your business and service.

First, I know which neighbors are leaving at 7:00–7:30 every morning and having to carry their sleepy children to the car. I'm assuming they are headed to a babysitter or daycare. Would these parents be open to learning about a stay-at-home opportunity?

Second, I see that a couple of my neighbors are day care providers as I see cars pulling up and dropping off children. Would the day-care mom or some of her customers need my product/service/opportunity?

Third, my best friend recently began working with a company focused on wellness. I found great leads for him as I see who else cares about their health because they are also walking. One guy even works out on his treadmill in his garage while watching the morning news program—great leads for this type of business.

Fourth, I notice yard signs from high schoolers announcing their position on the football team/cheer squad. Do these groups need a fundraiser?

Fifth, I see who is moving in and who is moving out. Do those moving out know I can continue to service them? As new people move in am I taking them a "welcome packet" complete with a token gift, sample, or gift certificate?

Sixth, I see who has brand new cars for sale. Could these people have overextended themselves with a car payment? Do I have a money making opportunity for them? Does my company have a car incentive program?

Seventh, look at what's in the trash. This sounds funny, but you can get to know a lot about people by what things they are throwing out. Please know I don't go picking through peoples' garbage–after all, I'm walking briskly! But, I know who has a new baby or expecting one because they have a playpen box on the curb. I see who has kids because of boxes from toys. I know who just bought new exercise equipment. Maybe someone just began a direct sales business and their empty kit box is being thrown out.

These are just seven ideas that you can do *TWISTS* on. Go for a walk, go at different times of day, get to know your neighbors, observe how you can service them with your product/ service/opportunity, or just be a good friend and neighbor. We all need more of that in our busy lives.

Here's to your fiscally fit business!

For other tips on working in your own backyard, refer to *The Lemon Aid Lead Alphabet: Where to Find Customers when you run out of Family and Friends,* pages 28-30–Door to Door; 43-44–Garage Sales; page 55–Home Owners Associations, pages 74-75– Neighborhoods; page 80–New People in the Area; pages 101-103–Telephone Books; page 109–Welcome Baskets; page 114–Yard Signs

Write the Right Stuff

As you continue to move Forward in your business, you'll want to Write the Right Stuff! Were you ever "punished" by a schoolteacher and had to write "sentences?" I remember getting in trouble for chewing gum, so I had to write: "I will not chew gum at school" one hundred times. Talk about negative writing! And it happens all the time. If I were a schoolteacher, I'd have students write, "I promise to abide by the classroom rules" one hundred times. After all, our subconscious is very powerful and it doesn't recognize the words "I will not." It only hears "chew gum at school." So, does this really change behavior?

As we go forward in our business, let's write some positive, specific sentences aimed at achieving a goal. Here are some quick ideas:

• I call ten people every day and book at least two parties.
• I am a team leader by November 30.
• I have qualified for the cruise to the Bahamas
• I hand out ten business cards a day and in return get names of ten new customers.

Let me illustrate how powerful this is. I had a big goal that I really, really wanted and had worked very hard for. I had accomplished the "qualifications" but needed to wait for an opening in the organization. I had no control over the latter part. On a card I wrote: I am promoted by January of 1995." Guess when I got the notification? December 29, 1994. Since that time, I have used the power of the pen to write and achieve my goals.

Some people suggest writing your goals on the infamous 3x5 card and read them every day. Since I'm the Lemon Aid Lady, I'll do a *TWIST* on that idea: Write your goal every day! The goal goes from your head to your heart to your hand to the pen and on to the paper. This is power–but it's not magic. You can't just write this down and then sit down and do nothing. But every time the ink hits the paper and you see the goal, you'll feel the goal, and your hands, feet, and heart work toward it as your subconscious guides you.

This positive writing works so well, it's almost scary! Get out the pen and paper, write your goal, and chew some gum while you're at it.

1. Multiply Your Business–then Divide

Business Math. Those two words make me cringe! I am not a math whiz! In fact, one of my fears about becoming a leader in a direct sales business was that I'd have to calculate figures. If you have someone on your team who is hesitating about advancing in the business, see if she/he might have the same fear!

I can do the basics: add, subtract, multiply, divide. So, here's a Math Quiz for you: Which is the easier equation:

First choice: $1 + 1 = 2$, $2 + 1 = 3$, $3 + 1 = 4$, $4 + 1 = 5$, $5 + 1 = 6$, $6 + 1 = 7$, $7 + 1 = 8$, $8 + 1 = 9$.

Second Choice: $3 \times 3 = 9$

Even I can figure out that multiplying is a whole lot easier–and faster–than adding one at a time.

How does that relate to your business? Are you adding to your business or multiplying? Adding is when you book, say three shows a week, every week in a month for a total of 12.

Multiplying is where you hold 12 shows in October and recruit four of the hostesses so that in November you hold another 12 and benefit from 12 more (each new recruit holds at least 3 shows in November) for a total of 24.

In November, you recruit four more of your hostesses, and your new consultants each recruit one of theirs. In December, you personally hold 12, but benefit from 12 of your October recruits, 12 from their recruits (each holding 3), and 12 from your November recruits for a total of 48. Doesn't that sound better than you trying to do it all yourself? I realize this is a "dream team". Not everyone holds 3 a month. So, cut that 48 in half–you're still multiplying your efforts!

2. Now, if you really want to multiply...ya gotta DIVIDE!
You know that $3 \times 3 = 9$. But let's do a *TWIST*. When 9 is divided by 3, the answer is 3 (I'm really getting smart!).
In your business, you've got to divide to multiply: Let's say you have nine team members. Three of them become leaders like you by recruiting five new consultants each–now you're dividing!. With their team members you have nearly thirty in your down line. Wasn't that even easier than multiplying?

You probably agree with me but are wondering "how to" multiply (in other words, how do I get more consultants and leaders in my organization?). You have a lot of "math teachers" in you life: your sponsor, leader, and company. If you still need some tutoring, stay tuned to the Lemon Aid List...

As you go forward in business—do the math: Multiplying and dividing is much more fun for everyone than simply adding.

Hostess Huddle vs. Hostess Coaching
Fall. The beginning of the best selling season of the year for party plan demonstrators! Fall is also kickoff time for football. When I think of watching a football game on TV, a picture of the coach on the sideline yelling at the players, "motivating" them to win the game comes to my mind. The coach has to be very serious and stern; after all, he has a game to win!

As a party plan professional, every time I use the term "hostess coaching" the same picture comes to my mind: a serious, stern coach. This past summer as I've been out in the field holding parties with a few Lemon Aid customers, I cringed whenever I said the word hostess "coaching."

After examining what a consultant and a hostess talk about in this session, I've done a *TWIST* and am suggesting we use another name for this very important, informal meeting using another football term: *Hostess Huddle.*

As a Party Plan Professional, the best way to have a more successful party, is to be one of the players, not simply a coach. This conclusion is drawn on my experiences as both a consultant holding an average of six parties a week, to–more importantly–my privileges of hosting parties in my own home. The consultants who have held demonstrations at my home taught me (yes, I still learn from everyone and plan to always do so) the best way is for all people involved in the party to be players.

How do we huddle with our hostesses? Just handing them an envelope with catalogs, order forms, and information is not enough. A quick phone call to be sure the envelope has arrived is also not sufficient. Nor is spending a quick few minutes at the party where the new hostess booked from.

I believe we need to plan about a 15-20 minute conversation (phone is fine as face-to-face might be difficult to schedule) for our "huddle" time! Here's what you'll want to accomplish:

1. Discover why she booked with you. This is what is going to move her to action. Although a Hostess Gift program is a great incentive, it's not everyone's reason for booking. Maybe she wants to show off her newly remodeled home. Perhaps she wants an excuse to make her famous pies. Ask her…this is really the key to knowing more about her and what her needs are.

2. What does she want you to show, tell, teach about and sell at her party? What specific ideas does she want to learn at her event? When you decide this, you'll be able to give her some "inviting words" to use (stay tuned to the list to learn about this concept). She needs to have a reason to call her friends to invite them so she doesn't feel like the party is all about her. If a hostess doesn't know the right words, she doesn't make the calls–except to call you to say "no one is coming; I'll have to cancel." Please refer to *Presentations for Profit$*, pages 61-68.

3. What kinds of gifts does she want to be delivered with her order? Those hostesses who book to earn specific items are generally the best hostesses. Not everyone is so definitive. If she says, "I'll wait to see how it goes," you can reply, "Pretend I'm giving you a gift certificate… do you want a $10, $25, $50, or $100?" This puts the goal in dollar terms. Now, show her what it takes to get that.

Or, if she's doesn't verbalize an exact product ask which products are her favorite. Does she have all the accessories for products that she already owns? Refer back to what products you'll be bringing to show, tell, teach about and sell. Would she like some of these items to have a permanent place in her home? These items are usually those she is wishing for, even if she doesn't convey her goal.

4. Encourage her to put a new message on her voice mail boxes at home and on her cellular phone (See *Presentations for Profit$,* page 2).

5. Ask if she's willing to read a paragraph or two (that you'll have prepared) to introduce you to her guests. See *Presentations for Profit$* pages 53-55).

6. Read off categories on the Top 40 List that you've prepared. Have her tell you who she knows in each category. By the time you've completed this exercise, her guest list will be nearly complete. Rather than putting this in the Hostess envelope, use it as a guide in your conversation to ask her which of her friends fit the categories.

This part of the huddle helps you to know information about the people she's inviting. You'll find who has extra needs or talents. This is the most important part of the huddle. You can even write the names, addresses, and phone numbers as she dictates to you. This is one sure way to get the list. (See *Presentations for Profit$* pages 3-6).

7. **Be sure she understands how to collect outside orders and payments**. Request she have all orders together on the day of her party so the order can be placed immediately and delivered in a timely manner (I know…this step isn't so easy!).

8. Present her with a great present: The company opportunity brochure or video.

I've found that most people (including me!) do not read the paperwork in the hostess envelope unless each piece is explained. This is why the "huddle" is so much more effective. You're planning the party together. You're both players on the same–not opposing–team. You're not on the sidelines yelling commands at her and stomping your feet when plays aren't done correctly (figuratively speaking, of course!).

And when you take the time to "huddle" you know she has things underway. After you do the "huddle" and keep in touch throughout the party process, she'll feel your true caring and the "huddle" becomes a "cuddle" for all involved.

Here's to many, many happy Hostess Huddles!

A Child Shall Lead Us

My husband is so kind and soft hearted. Everyone who comes to our door selling anything gets an order from him. I come home from trips to find candy bars, frozen cookie dough, maps, magazines, and other items he purchased to help out the neighborhood kids in their school fundraising endeavors.

The other day, however, he was engaged in a project and couldn't stop to visit with the young man. He invited the young solicitor to come back when "my wife is home." A couple evenings later while working in my office, I heard the doorbell ring. Since both my kids had gone to work, I stopped writing and answered the door. The young solicitor had returned. And he taught me some lessons I want to pass on to you:

1. He left his house. I was actually surprised to see this kid. I thought with our security-conscious society that we didn't allow kids to go door-to-door. We're adults. We think going door-to-door to visit customers is unsafe and absurd. Do you know how many doors of opportunity you're missing? He also returned! He didn't take my husband's "come back when my wife is home" as a NO! How often do we hear, "Call me later" and never do; we assume the person is using that as a polite way to say no.

2. He visited with me in person. Many people tell me stories of how they have left their catalogs at hundreds (literally!) of houses. When I ask if they met the people, I hear only that they just left the literature. Your catalogs are not you. You must see people face to face. You are the best representation of your product. He was also excited about what he was selling and knew the products. I was surprised at the variety of items in the fund raiser catalog. He told me about different ones and which were the best. He was interested in me and gave me suggestions on what to purchase.

3. He had a goal. He wanted to win the fancy radio in the sales contest. He needed to sell 110 items to win it and he was determined to win. When I looked at his sales sheet, he had only sold ten items; thirteen with my order. But he didn't seem discouraged. He pleasantly told me about his goal.

4. He kept track of his activity. I noticed on the sales sheet that there wasn't anyplace to put my address. I wondered how he would know how to get my merchandise to me. He pulled out a sheet of lined paper. On this sheet were the addresses of everyone in our subdivision. Next to each address, he had written comments like "Can't buy now," "Come back when wife is home," "Eating dinner." Smart kid. Do we keep track of our daily activities so we can FOLLOW THROUGH?

5. I sure wish the school would have had a fund raiser with one of YOUR companies!

Midterm Exam

It's "Midterm" on the Back-to-School/Forward-in-Business tips, and you can take the following "test" to see if your Family/Business/Personal priorities are in the right portions. You will grade your own answers:

1. Your hostess had a great demonstration. You really want to talk to her about joining your team, but she's a single career woman with no children. You decide to:

   a. Boldly tell her that your job is better than hers and she needs to sell your product.
   b. Be quiet about your opportunity. After all, direct sales businesses were created only for stay-at-home moms who need to get out of the house.
   c. Take time to explain the benefits of joining your team for people at all "slices of life."

2. Two of your children come down with a case of chicken pox on the same day that you have a demonstration scheduled. Your husband is out of town. What do you do:

   a. Get a babysitter and go to the demonstration.
   b. Call the hostess and cancel the demonstration.
   c. Have another consultant do the demonstration for you.

3. Your monthly sales meeting is next Thursday. On the soccer team schedule, you notice next Thursday is your turn to car pool for your daughter's practice:

   a. You tell your daughter you have to go to the meeting; she'll have to miss practice.
   b. Stay home from the meeting and drive the car pool.
   c. Trade driving days with another mom.

4. You're all excited to get your business on the grow. As a single mom of three teen-aged kids and holding a full-time job–you're just not sure how you can do it all, so you:

   a. Hold demonstrations every night on the way home from work and let the kids take care of themselves.
   b. Hope people will call you to book classes at your house so you don't ever have to leave home.
   c. Share your vision of your home-based business with your kids. Designate days to build your business and delegate responsibilities to your kids for those days.

5. It's 9:30 p.m. You've just returned from one of your best demonstrations. As soon as you get home, you:

    a. Call your leader and share your exciting success, then you talk for another hour or more.

    b. Catch up on today's soap operas that you video-taped earlier.

    c. Be sure your children are nestled in bed and then go nestle with your husband.

6. Your husband complains that you interrupt family time to accept business phone calls. You:

    a. Tell him that's what happens when you have a home-based business—get used to it.

    b. Take the phone off the hook except for two hours in a day.

    c. Get a separate phone line and phone number with voice mail. This way you can turn the ringer off when you don't want to take calls and your customers can have full access to you. You can return their calls without interrupting your family time.

7. You are employed full-time in addition to having your own business. You're looking forward to the day you can leave your full-time job to be home full time while growing your business. You:

    a. Keep trying to get your business income to match or exceed your full-time job income and then you'll quit your job.

    b. Quit your business until you retire from your full-time job.

    c. Calculate your income and subtract the expenses related to your job. Get a realistic figure of what your net income is (deduct child care, parking, lunch, gas, tolls, etc). Add in the unbuyable benefits: raising your kids yourself, less stress trying to focus on too many things.

8. You're excited for your demonstration tomorrow night. Then the hostess cancels due to a family emergency. You're disappointed so you:

    a. Go shopping at the mall.

    b. Take your kids to the park.

    c. Spend the time you would have been at the demonstration on the phone calling customers and future hosts and recruits.

9. You're overjoyed to learn you're expecting a baby. You:

    a. Cancel all business for a year.

    b. Plan two extra demonstrations a month and earmark the profits to buy baby supplies and equipment.

c. Are so thankful your home-based business allows you to work at your own pace. If your health stays good, you can work up to the birth and resume your business gradually as you feel is best.

10. Your recruiting efforts are paying off! Five new people have just joined your team. To give them a good start, you:

    a. Go to each person's home and teach them one-on-one.
    b. Have everyone meet at McDonalds with their kids. Tell them to review the manual and videos in their company kit.
    a. Invite them to attend a regularly-scheduled group orientation session at your home.

11. You have done extremely well in your business and are now out-earning your husband. You:

    a. Remind him every day how wonderful you are and that your income is more valuable than his.
    b. Hoard all your money in a separate checking account that only you have access.
    c. Invite him to join you as a full-time partner in your business so you can reap greater time and income benefits and strengthen your marriage.

12. You are at the end of your rope; combining the business and home has gotten out of hand. You feel you are not effective in either role, so you:

    a. Run away from home; you feel like your husband and kids will be better without you.
    b. Give up on the business and become a martyr.
    c. Do the Lemon Aid *TWIST*…use your family as your passion for strengthening your family and building business together—not as an excuse for giving up on either!

The correct anwer to all questions is "c." If raising a family, building a business, and/or working at another job has created a *Sour Situation* for you, attend the Lemon Aid Learning Adventure "Family Fortunes without Family Feuds."

Chapter Eleven: Fall – Celebrate the Harvest

What Cycle is Your Business On?

Do you love doing laundry? I find if I do a load a day, I'm not so bogged down with the chore. (Keep reading; this isn't a message about cleaning!) Have you ever paid attention to what your washing machine really does? It doesn't just wash. Mine fills with water, then after washing, it spins, drains, rinses, drains and spins again. It has more than one function, even though it's called a washing machine. In other words, in order to wash clothes, it has to cycle through other activities.

We've just finished summer. Time to get back to our plans and forward in our businesses. I've heard from many of you that this summer was a bit "dry" with regard to sales and bookings. We can examine and then analyze what happens in direct sales during the hot, dry summer or the cold, dreary, snowy winter–or any season for that matter. However, if we spend too much time to analyze, we paralyze. Let's just realize that like most things in life, our businesses go through cycles. Seasons turn from one to the other, night turns to day, people age…we all cycle. Examine your local garden center where you buy your flowers in the spring. What does this businessperson do in the winter? Is the center closed down? Some are, but the smart business owners do the *TWIST*. The Garden Centers become Christmas Tree Farms. Landscapers who mowed your lawn in the summer, shovel your snow in the winter. Life is cyclic; we decide what activities to do in those cycles to keep the business moving.

Direct sales companies market products via home demonstration and/or one-on-one appointments. If we're in a cycle where we need a *TWIST* to keep going, we can also do corporate presentations, fundraisers, booths at home shows or fairs, preschool displays… and the list goes on and on. Every season has its reason for people to say "no" to buying, booking, and selling. Our customers are cyclic; in every cycle, we'll have people who will and will not want to do business with us. A hostess has a time when she's ready to host, then a time she only wants to buy, and other times she doesn't even want to talk to us. The key is to keep working on other activities or with other people while we cycle through seasons and while our contacts go through their cycles. Having lots of different people at different stages of the business cycle is one way to have continual Sweet Successes and Juicy Profits. Whatever you do, don't stop working; complete the cycle.

What would happen if you opened your washer and discovered it quit after the washing cycle and hadn't rinsed yet? First, you'd get mad, kick it a few times (sometimes that works!), then call a repairperson. Continue working on your business with *TWISTS* according to the cycles of the seasons and customers desires. Life Cycles. And so does business. I'm just waiting for the cycle on my dryer to fold the clothes and put them away!

Doughnut Week

Have you had a "Sippin' Cider, Sit Beside Her" time with your team? Thanks for the feedback many of you have sent! What is the best thing to have with cider? How about doughnuts? Here's another team-building week: "DOUGHNUT WEEK". This is also known as optimism week. Why? Because when you look at a doughnut, what letter does it resemble? An "O" for OPTIMISM (if you've attended a Lemon Aid Seminar you know this is part of the Lemon Aid "Ahhh Haaaa Alphabet"!). This is the week to stay focused on all the good things you do individually, as a team, and as a representative of your company. Kick off the week by treating everyone to doughnuts. If you live at a distance, see if a grocery store sells doughnut coupons (Albertsons does this for Halloween; they are very inexpensive, and easy to mail). Attach this saying to the doughnut: "As you go through life, an important thing to know: Keep your eye upon the DOUGHNUT and not upon the HOLE!" The message in this message is often we look at what we don't have, what we haven't accomplished, etc. This is the week to stay OPTIMISTIC and acknowledge all that is great! An added idea: Doughnut begins with "do." Doing is the beginning of accomplishing goals. So go out and DOUGHNUT !

Bag of Recruiting Tricks—and Treats

This is the week you can put Recruiting in the Bag–the Trick or Treat Bag that is! Carry a Trick or Treat Bag with you everywhere you go. Announce to everyone both at and away from your demonstrations:

T he
R eason
I
C an
K eep

O n
R ecruiting (or "Reaching my Goals")

T ime (not only do I choose the TIME I work, but I also choose the TIME I get paid, how much TIME I want to work, and have more quality TIME)

R elationships (I can renew and extend my RELATIONSHIPS. Renew with my family and friends, and extend my circle of business friends and customers)

E conomics (I have control over my own ECONOMIC situation. I don't worry about lay-offs or downsizing. I have employment insurance!)

A dvance (I choose when and how fast I ADVANCE in my business. I don't have to wait for someone to retire or die! And, with advancements come pay increases and other tangible and intangible benefits.

T each customers how to use my products. Teach others how to build a busines. I can be *your* teacher.

Your Advancement to Teacher

Did you ever have a teacher who did your homework? I sure didn't. But I had many teachers who taught me well so I could accomplish my assignments. I've discovered in my 23 plus years with party plans that we tend to be helpers–not teachers; I include myself in this group.

When I had a prospective hostess or consultant with concerns about hosting or joining, the words out of my mouth were "I'll help you." I discovered that many people interpreted that as "I'll do it for you":

• "I'll help you get bookings" meant, "I'll book parties for you."
• "I'll help you plan a successful show" meant, "I'll do all the work."

When I learned the *TWIST*, by changing a couple of words, my team and bookings grew. The words were simply, "I'll *teach* you how to schedule classes" or "I'll *teach* you how to have a fun party." Teaching goes far beyond helping. The "word" teach implies that the other person has a responsibility as well. Teaching others also sharpens our teaching skills and we become better teachers.

Your next role as a teacher: Have you ever heard someone say, "I can't join your company– I'm just not a salesperson." My reply: "I'm not looking for sales people. I'm looking for people who love my product and have a passion for teaching others how to use it.

Now, the last way to look at teaching: Have you ever received a brochure for Adult or Continuing Education? Years ago, when I was still unsure about my role as a home party demonstrator, I was reading through the classes offered in my community. I realized each time I went to someone's home for a home party, I was teaching them many of the ideas that people were paying money for in these classes. My value increased a hundredfold. I realized I wasn't charging people to come to the demonstration (if you work with a company that does charge you already have realized the value) and yet the guests always learned and had a lot of fun! Value what you have to offer, be sure your demonstrations are full of fun and valuable information, and as you teach others, not simply "help" them, your business–and value–will also increase. You've heard the adage, "The more you learn, the more you earn." Here's my Lemon Aid *TWIST*: "The more you teach, the more you sell."

Mixed Up About Recruiting? Here's a Recipe.

Here's a Recruiting Recipe you can use at your demonstrations–even if your product has nothing to do with food preparation. We all love to eat, and everyone wants more $$$. This is a fun way to present your opportunity. This is also a great recipe to use at the BOO Opportunity Meeting you'll find (along with the OpportuniTREE Opportunity Meeting) in the *Lemon Aid Sweet Holiday Success* CD and FREE Bonus Booklet.

We all Win Halloween Mix

2 cups candy corn	1 cup salted peanuts
1 cup M&Ms®	1 cup Apple Jack® cereal

Mix all together in a fun Halloween Bowl (incorporate your product, of course). You can also put some in small, decorated bags to give as a take home treat with a company brochure. Give only to those who are curious about learning more.

At your party or BOO Opportunity Meeting, explain the mix like this:

"Are you mixed up wondering how you're going to pay for Christmas gifts this year? (A new car, kids clothes, etc.) Here's a mix that could be the answer. If you like to have fun and are a little "nutty" [peanuts], consider beginning your own business with _____. You can decide how many zeroes [Apple Jacks] you want in the dollar part of your check: 1.00, 100.00, 1,000, 10,000.00, etc. In our business, you'll be able to Make Money [M&Ms] at least three ways: [show candy corn with the three colors and apply specifically to your business].

1. Commissions by selling product is at the base of our business
2. Sponsoring other people to begin their own business is next
3. For those who want to "point" their way to the top, you have the potential for leadership bonuses.

If you're curious about *TWISTING* your mix up into money, let's get together so I can tell you about more treats!"

Please note how I'm using the word "curious" rather than interested. Most people are not interested until they have more information. They request more information when their curiosity is aroused. Go find some *curious* people to share your mix–and business–with! Other words: No longer will you be "scared" of a "witchy" boss, black cat crossing your path, or other spooks! Your new career and success can be in the bag–the Trick or Treat Bag! For those who are very interested, fill up small paper Trick or Treat bags. Put some recruiting information and a couple of treats inside to leave with her/him.

Chapter Twelve: Thanksgiving and Gratitude

Be Grateful for the Opportunity

Have you been feasting on "How to Win Friends (and hostesses and customers)" when you do the *TWIST*? Here's the story I promised about how a couple strengthened their very good marriage, which could have been headed for trouble because of criticism. As you read this, think of how you can *TWIST* this idea into building your family and business.

This is the story about my very best friend. He was going through some rough, challenging times. He had a left a decent job to purchase a business that he and his wife had dreamed of owning. They planned on building the business and then selling it upon retirement in 15 to 20 years. Unfortunately, the business was not their dream; rather more of a nightmare, and they sold it. Now, my friend was out in the job market–again. He had done well as a professional previous to the business fiasco, but now had a very difficult time securing a job. He did whatever jobs he could get to support his wife and children. In the meantime, his wife had an opportunity to take some college courses. She, too, was undecided about her future career plans, and this opportunity came at a golden time.

Additionally, her children attended school near the college, about an hour from their home. My friend is a very kind, caring, thoughtful husband to his wife. However, she began to be critical of many of his actions. While she was at school during the day, he did household chores, prepared dinner, and every morning he made his wife a lunch to take to school along with a glass of juice in her commute cup. His wife would criticize that the dinner could have been prepared in a better manner, that she didn't like tomatoes in her salad for lunch, and so on. The husband seemed to let all this roll off his back. He continued to do little acts of kindness and was always considerate of his wife, even though he was experiencing personal uncertainty and, at times, depression because of the lack of employment—now going on a year.

Fortunately, my friend's wife remembered what she had read in Dale Carnegie's book (this is why I'm using this story) about avoiding criticism and giving appreciation. She decided if she didn't start to show appreciation, she might not have a husband to appreciate. Their twentieth wedding anniversary was approaching. She had an idea for the best gift...one that wouldn't cost any money, which was good since they had none. It was the beginning of May; their anniversary was June 22. She had to get busy complimenting and looking for all the good things her husband had done and did every day and then...she wrote them in a journal entitled "How do I love thee...let me count the ways." Her goal was to write 20 ways every day. She spent the time in her car right after class remembering all the acts of kindness her husband had done in the previous 24 hours for her–and others (he was a good man to everyone). She wrote down things she had never noticed before: "You listen to me give you directions." "You shook the kitchen rugs." "You put your arm around me when we drive." "You encourage me." "You love rain." On their anniversary, her husband was really touched by this "unbuyable" gift. This was the turning point for this couple. Many couples are torn apart during times of uncertainty. This gift – a gift of appreciation – helped this couple cleave together. This year they will celebrate 25 years of love...and appreciation.

Create a Horn of Plenty

This is the week to create your own "Horn of Plenty" business. The first step is to get on the "horn" (telephone) and make "plenty" of calls! As you fill up your Horn with new hostesses and recruits, you will create a "home of plenty." Plenty of time with your family without feeling guilty that you're not working your business and plenty of resources to provide for your family. And of course, PLENTY of new friends and business...

So, get on the HORN for PLENTY of new business!

Thanksgiving Day

Today is Thanksgiving Day in Canada! But, everyday can be Thanksgiving Day everywhere. And, if you want to keep committed customers, THANK THEM. Here's an idea to watch your business grow as you give thanks. Decide how many shows/parties/presentations you want between now and December 31. Purchase that amount of Thank you notes (or, make them yourself using stamp products from our direct sales friends!).

In addition to the note that you'll write WHEN THE SHOW IS SCHEDULED...not after it's held (send one then, too!), enclose one of the reminder magnets from Jenny B's Booster (http://thebooster.com or call her office at 1-800-5JENNYB). These magnets come four to a sheet and are very inexpensive. The ones I've used say "It's your Party" "It's your Show"...she has others, too. On these magnets is a place to write your name, phone, company, and demonstration date. Your hostess will have a reminder of YOU and YOUR BUSINESS and date of your show/party/demo every time she opens the fridge. And she'll keep it. Pile these note cards and magnets somewhere where you'll see them EVERY DAY. Is the pile shrinking every day? By the first part of December, you shouldn't have any left, because you've sent your thanks out. In return, hostesses do have better shows and the best part is when you thank them, you keep them!

Chapter Thirteen: Christmas

We Need a Little Christmas, Right Now

Last Sunday after church, I pulled in my driveway and noticed how festive our neighborhood was looking. My good friend next door had her mailbox decorated with a simple red bow...what a nice contrast to our green mail boxes. And, she had her wreaths on the garage lights. Are you all decorated for Christmas? I started a week ago and am still hanging holly, garland, lights, and other ornaments. As I was fluffing up some of my garland, I thought how these decorations are stored for so long and enjoyed for such a short time. Then my thoughts turned to customers; sometimes we only see them once a year – like our Christmas decorations.

We're always excited to pull our festive fixin's out of the boxes and display them. Just like we're excited to renew acquaintances with customers we haven't seen in a while. I have one problem. I can't find my box with the wreaths. I'm sure it's in the attic; if I'd just take a minute and go up there, I know I'd see the box marked "wreaths." It's taking that minute. And if I don't do that soon, the holidays will be over and my garage lights and front door will remain bare. Do you have any customers you've been meaning to call? You know they're there, you're sure they'd be happy to hear from you, but it's just taking that time. I have a holiday challenge for you...and a gift. The challenge is to call some of those people. If you don't know whom to call, how about calling all your *Hollies*. Sometimes it takes some "fluffing," so pick up the phone right now and punch in the numbers.

Then call your *Marys*; you may be losing faith, so dial the number right now. For these people need your products, want to see your demo, need to buy some more gifts; hurry now and call them. They want you to remember that they love your service; they need a little contact. Now, call *everybody*...put out the word before your fingers forget to dial. Fill up your date books, we've no time for putting off all these calls but hostesses are waiting for you to call.

What's in Santa's Bag?

One huge benefit of representing a direct sales company, specifically one which offers hostess gifts, is that you get to be Santa (or Mrs. Santa) all year long! You give gifts all year long...and things people want because they choose their gifts. What fun! When I made goals for the week/month/quarter, I focused on how many $$$ of product could I GIVE rather than how much could I sell. What a difference it made to tell people, "I'm going to give away $2,000 in _____ this month. How much of it do you want?" Remember what I said, people chose what they wanted. Would it be as fun if you just gave a hostess a pre-packed gift without asking her what she wanted? Even though the surprise element is there, most people like to choose their gifts, kind of like writing a Santa list...it's always nice to get what you really want and didn't think you'd get it.

Sweet Successful Holiday Treats

Here's an SWEET, SUCCESSFUL recipe for SIMPLE caramels. Enjoy your holiday week and the baker's dozen of Lemon Aid Ideas! (This recipe is so easy is delicious, I hope you and your waistline don't mind!):

1/2 cup butter (not margarine)	1/2 cup white sugar
1/2 cup sweetened condensed milk	1/2 cup white corn syrup
1/2 cup brown sugar	1/2 cup chopped pecans, if desired (Texas pecans!)

Melt butter in 1 quart microwaveable bowl. Add sugars, syrup, and milk. Stir well and microwave for 6-8 min. Pour into buttered 8" x 8" dish and refrigerate 30 min. Cut into pieces. If too firm to cut, warm in the microwave seconds at a time until desired consistency is reached. Wrap pieces in waxed paper.

Chapter Fourteen: Avoid the Holiday Blues in Your Business

Take a Winner To Lunch

Here's a fun idea that I've been using at my Lemon Aid Learning Adventures: A way to build your business with Business Cards, with a *TWIST,* of course! At your product presentations, rather than doing the, same-old door prize drawings, try this: a Business Card Drawing. Invite each guest to give you one of her business cards for a drawing. On the back of the card, have her code it in one of three ways: B: She wants to BUY your product on a regular basis. G: She wants GIFTS by being a hostess S: She wants to SELL; you SHARE your business with her. Why is this effective? First, no extra writing for the guest...this is SIMPLE! Oh, you're asking, "What if she doesn't have a business card?"

This is a great opportunity for the both of you. Have extras of your own or blank cards. Invite her to design her own card and career. She can give herself any title, just be sure her name, phone, and address are on the card. And, while she's designing her card, she can write what hours she would work and how much she wants to get paid for her career (of course the career can be mom, homemaker, etc.). This is a great recruiting tool, do your own *TWISTS* on this. Second, without having to ask a lot of questions, you'll have INFORMATION about your guests—where she works, what her position is, etc.

Now, do your typical drawing for what you usually give away, but, with a *TWIST*, of course! You are going to keep those cards throughout the month. After you've collected business cards at all your presentations (as well as from others you meet during the month), you'll do a monthly drawing for a free lunch where YOU WILL TAKE YOUR CUSTOMER TO LUNCH! This is a really fun way to get to know your customers, develop stronger relationships, and share your business opportunity. Recently, I took October's winner (Kim from Home Interiors and Gifts) out for a delightful lunch. I even helped her schedule a presentation with the waitress. She couldn't believe how easy that was!

Sweet Holiday Recruiting Idea

Here's the first of the Baker's Dozen of Lemon Aid Ideas: Purchase candy canes in bulk (they are inexpensive now and available!) Attach a little note to each one that reads something like this:

"Are you a bit wobbly about your future? Call _____ (your name) at ___ _____ (phone) You can lean on me to support you in a new business adventure with _____ (your company)."

How do you use this? Carry them in your purse/briefcase (careful so they don't break).

As you're out and about preparing for the holidays give these to people you meet who you'd like to work with. For example, standing in lines, in elevators, at school Christmas programs, to retail employees, the people who deliver newspapers/packages/mail to your home...

Strike up a conversation by saying, "I have a Christmas gift for you (this gets their attention)." Continue, "This candy cane only represents a gift I'm offering: an opportunity with my company, _____ (name of your company)."

Remember: only give the gift in exchange for the person's name/phone so you can follow through. Will everyone say, "yes" to joining your team? Of course not, but you now have a crutch (or should I say "cane") to use to create curiosity—all while you're out and about!

Holiday Sandwich Shows

The beauty of having our own business is we get to take the holidays off, right? However, do you realize that a really big week for home parties is the week "sandwiched" in between Christmas and New Years? Why? A lot of people are on vacation, they have relatives in, they are more relaxed, they have Christmas money to spend, they already have food galore for refreshments, they are in a festive mood and want to keep celebrating...and on and on. Why don't more people host more demonstrations? They simply have not been asked! So, my second of the baker's dozen ideas is this: Schedule a Sandwich Show—sandwiched in between these two major holidays. If your customers have vacation, consider doing daytime events. Use the "sandwich" theme to draw larger attendance.

The Winter Workshop

Another great activity during "Sandwich Week" (the week between Christmas and New Year's) is to have a team Winter Workshop. This was a tradition with my team, and we held it during this week. After Christmas, we all had a little "cabin fever."

Kids/Company/Spouses are home and can entertain themselves with their Christmas gifts while Mom reconnects with her sales team. The event was very informal; however, it was planned. Dress was casual; refreshments are optional. Normally our Winter Workshop went from 6:00–9:00 p.m. Team members all participated by attending and/or presenting. This was definitely a "hands on" event. If you sell stamps or scrapbooks, great time to demonstrate a project. Personal makeovers for our friends who sell skin care. Cooking classes if you sell kitchen products. Decorators can put together showpieces. Instead of just being "shown" something, this is a time to actually "do." If you haven't created your purse/pocket presentations (*Lemon Aid Lead Alphabet,* page 84) this is a wonderful opportunity to do this. I liken this Winter Workshop to an old-fashioned quilt bee. Everyone is busy learning, doing, and connecting. You can also do mini classes and rotate every hour or so (similar to the "Back to School" ideas in *Totally Terrific Team Theme* book.) Keep your Winter Workshop low-keyed, fun, and easy and this event will become a tradition with your team to give a great beginning to the New Year!

Money Grows on Christmas Trees

Our mothers taught us that money does not grow on trees. However, you do have a tree where money does grow–it's your OpportuniTREE. This is the season for Christmas trees. Watch for small tree items at craft stores or tree-shaped candy. At your demonstrations, and as you're out and about, talk to people about your OpportuniTREE. After you've given them a short advertisement (less than two minutes), give them an OpportuniTREE to remember your conversation. Then ask, "When do you want to see the money start to grow?" You see, your business is like a tree. You and your company are the roots. Your hostesses are the branches; customers are the leaves and fruit. As customers are converted to hostesses, more branches are added. (Or, recruits can be represented by branches; you choose how to present this). Have fun sharing your Christmas OpportuniTREE this season.

Chapter Fifteen: Why We Work

Why We Work, Level One

There's a question you should always ask yourself if you want to expand a business—WHY? Not "why" should you ask the question, but WHY are you taking action to grow an enterprise.

You might have begun because of the prospect of financial rewards or because you are a fan of a product. These could be one of the reasons you began, but what is your underlying reason why you work? In the next five messages, we'll examine the five reasons we take action on working in our businesses, or any endeavor for that fact.

As humans, we want positive things in our lives, but we're too focused on the negative–in other words, we're afraid. The fear could be fear of not providing for our family, so we go to work, even if we don't like what we do for a living. Perhaps the negative drive you have is because you don't want your family and friends to say, "I told you so" if you don't achieve your desired results.

Could this negative focus also cause you to get on the phone and call customers? I know so. As I was making calls one day, a customer said she had just booked a party with another consultant. What did I do? I worked even more feverishly...I wanted to be sure none of my other customers abandoned me (when in fact I had abandoned her by not keeping in better touch!).

Often I worked in earnest because I was afraid if I didn't work. I might have to go work in a negative environment—for someone else. I was a consistent performer because I didn't want my children raised by others so I made sure my income far exceeded that of being an employee.

Can fear cause one to take action? You bet! Self-inflicted negativity works as does the fear factor placed on us by others. I identify this Why We Work (WWW) Level as Level One: "N" for **Negative**. We might be working on this "N" level if we fear that if we aren't consistent we won't earn the incentive trip.

Look at the reason "why" you put efforts into you business. Is this a bad thing to work for fear that you won't acquire something? No...if it puts us to work, it works. Some people are paralyzed by fear...that's a whole other story. That's their reason not to work. If your reason to work is because you don't want Negative results in your life—fear, and it works, good for you. However, stay tuned to the next four messages as I share four other levels of why we work.

Why We Work, Level Two

The second WWW is represented by an "O," **Other's Opinions**: The opinions of others include recognition we get when we do a great job. It's being recognized by your leader/company/co-worker. And it feels good ! Maybe you work because when you do, your leader sends a note in the mail and it's the only envelope you get that doesn't have a window in it, rather it contains priceless, winning words.

This can also refer to your family and friends giving you accolades for what you do. The recognition can come from anyone; when you work at this level it's because other people notice what you do…and give you praise. The praise is like oil to a car engine; it keeps you moving!

Have you ever worked so hard to be a top performer you didn't even realize how much money you were making? All you cared about was being recognized at convention and receiving the glory, not just the gift! In my quest to be recognized at conferences, I achieved many goals I would not have had the opinions of others not been important to me. Other people spurring you on can turn you on to your work!

Do you see why recognition on stage at the annual convention or simply sending a congratulations card to one of your team members can be the WWW in someone's life? Recognition, the "**Opinions of Others**" is a great level to be at when you're looking at Why We Work.

Why We Work, Level Three

As we climb the levels of Why We Work, have you noticed that each level begins with a letter of the alphabet? After you read this message, write down the letters I've shared with you so far. "N" was first; "O" was second. If you were to write the letters as you would climb a ladder, the first letter (N) goes on the bottom rung and we build from there. Do you know which word I'm spelling?

Today's letter is "M" for monetary rewards–**Money**. This third level may be one of the major reasons "Why We Work" each day to build our businesses–even if we don't want to admit it! **Money** is a consistent measurement of our efforts. In other words, it's the tangible reward we receive from our efforts. The fun thing is we can exchange the reward to obtain other items!

If we work at Level Two (the Opinions of Others), because our goal is to be top seller on our team, the measurement can be skewed because we're using the performance of others as a measuring device. When we work at Level Three, we have *a more accurate measurement that can be saved, spent, or invested!* Sounds like a good level to me!

Speaking of measuring money, did you know a dollar bill is approximately 6" long? If you have a customer wondering the size of a product shown in the catalog, one you don't have for display, rather than using your fingers or arms to illustrate, pull out some bills! And then you can do the *TWIST*...and say, "The candle is about as tall as these two $20.00 bills are wide. Speaking of $20.00...I average at least five of these at every show!" This will surely get attention. And, every time a customer pulls out a dollar bill to measure something, whom will she remember? You !

Working on Level Three–"M"–is a good idea! Is there anything wrong with working at this level? Of course not. Just remember these messages are not to *tell you* the level to be in your WWW, but rather they are to help you assess if the levels you're working at are getting you the best results.

Why We Work, Level Four

Our letter this week is "E" for **Expectations**. (Have you figured out the word being spelled?)

Regardless of our positions in life or business, we have **Expectations** placed on us–real or implied. If you are a sales leader, your **Expectations** could be spelled out in terms of sales volume to be produced on a monthly basis both personally and/or for your team. Perhaps your **Expectations** are to attend sales meetings and conventions on a regular basis. The Expectations of your position could be that you hold meetings and teach new people.

As a sales consultant, your **Expectations** might also be attached to personal volume and/or number of classes/workshops/parties held.

Rising to and exceeding such **Expectations** is characteristic of working at Level Four. Let me illustrate. A close acquaintance–I'll call him Bill–had a very important job at a very large, prestigious company. Yet in spite of his high pay, he hated his job. The hours were horrendous (70+ each week) and the work tedious and repetitive (same work, different client syndrome). He often threatened to quit! (Sound familiar?) But he kept performing above and beyond the **Expectations**. Why? Because he had committed to these **Expectations** upon his accepting employment. In return, the company compensated him very, very well in terms of dollars and other perks. And he, in return, worked harder and harder...until he was offered a position with another company.

He gave his first employer the appropriate notice and wondered if they'd have him leave immediately, as some companies do for security reasons. Instead, they wanted him to complete his projects and even offered him a promotion if he would stay. Now, he could have easily slacked off during those two weeks and done less than a half-satisfactory job. But, now he was committed to his own Expectations and worked faithfully to the end.

Did you get that last sentence? **"His own" Expectations**. *As we work because of the expectations of our position, our personal* **Expectations** *increase.* We look at "minimums" as the base of our performance, not as our maximum efforts. We work at this level out of self-respect through self-discipline.

On a personal level, those of us who are parents have the Expectation of our title to provide for the essential physical and emotional needs of our children. I would guess that most parents go well above the essential **Expectation** of the title and nurture, enjoy, teach, love, appreciate, recognize (to mention only a few) their children.

Where much is given, much is required, and this level is a stretch above the rest. Expectations don't exist with excuses. Being a leader, consultant, employee, or any other position you hold is not just a title–because the title comes with **Expectations**. If you get up in the morning and recognize the blessings and responsibilities of your opportunity and position, and work in spite of obstacles or excuses, you're working at Level Four. Look around...you'll probably find that you have little company up there. Most of your peers will be working at Levels One-Three.

You'll also notice that working at this level is not directly tied to the "ME" factor–what you're going to get. *Yet, when you DO work at this level of* **Expectations,** *you become entitled to greater rewards*–especially when you advance to Level Five.

Why We Work, Level Five

"L" represents the top, Level Five, of Why We Work: **LOVE!** We work because we absolutely **LOVE** what we do. In fact at this level, the verb "work" becomes synonymous with FUN, ENJOYMENT, PLEASURE, PASSION! We go to work because our work is part of who we are, not what we "have" to do.

Pure love eliminates pressure. We love what we do so much; we are so secure in our www that if people say no, if others don't approve of our activity, if we're not making enough money or receiving the recognition we feel we deserve, we do it anyway. Love transcends all the other levels.

In August of 2002, *USA Today* cited a survey done by McPheters & Company asking women what's most important about a man's job. Guess what? The top response was NOT money. Here are the results: 43% feel that having a man enjoy his job is the most important. Second, with 25%, was for him to provide for his family. Twenty percent said the job must have growth potential; ten percent wanted his job to benefit society, and two percent wanted perks for her. In other words, women feel the most important aspect of a man's job (and I believe a woman's job, too!) is that they **LOVE** what they do!

Love is the reason so many people *TWIST* their hobby into their full time work. They have a love and passion for something and they've discovered a way to profit financially from this love. Could you have begun your present business because you were in **LOVE** with the product and company? Are you still working at Level Five?

May I share a personal experience? I LOVE to teach! For as long as I can remember I have wanted to be a teacher. After school, when all my friends wanted the freedom to play out-of-doors, I went to the basement of our family home to a makeshift schoolroom in the corner of the laundry room. And there I would teach various "subjects" to either imaginary students, or my friends whom I'd cajoled into spending after school hours with me.

Because I love to teach, I have a passion for learning. And, as I learn about new ideas, products, and concepts, I want to open my mouth and tell others. As I result, my love of teaching became a love of selling because as I shared information about products and opportunities with others, I got paid for it! How amazing! The more I taught, the more people bought. The more they bought, the more they wanted to sell! And, the bigger my team grew. It all began with my love of teaching, which I continue to do today.

Do I work at Level Five every day? No. Some days I get distracted. Some days I'm tired. Some days I even get discouraged. I discovered a way to take my temperature as to what level I'm at. Maybe this will help you know what level you're working at so you can decide what level you want to be at. My temperature comes from the words I speak–mostly to myself–and the attitude I convey to others.

Level One: N – Negative; fear of what we'll lose if we don't work
"I *better* get on the phone and make calls."
"I *better* book some parties"
Can you feel the trepidation in these words….If I don't do a task, I won't get the results.

Level Two: O – Opinions of Others
"I've *got to* get on the phone or my leader will be mad."
"I've *got to* recruit or my team won't think I'm a good leader."

Level Three: M – Monetary Rewards
"I *need to* sell something so I can pay my mortgage."
"I *need to* make money or my spouse will make me quit the business."
"I *need to* earn the cruise so I can surprise my family."

Level Four: E – Expectations of our position leading to Expectations of ourselves
"I *want to* share my business with others because someone shared with me."
"I *want to* call my customers because they will be thrilled to hear the news about..."
"I *want to* attend our conventions so I can be the best at what I do."

Level Five: L – Love

"I *love to* hold team meetings so I can teach, recognize, and inspire my team."

"I *love to* visit with prospects about joining our company because what I offer can benefit their lives."

"I *love to* call my customers so I can service them according to their wishes."

• What words are you saying to yourself as you begin to work on building your business?

• Do you work out of obligation or because of your passion?

• Do you work so others will praise you or so that you can support your family?

Remember, the higher the WWW levels, the loftier your reason for working. However, as long as you do work and reach your goals, the level you work at is totally up to you. I believe the greater satisfaction for you, your customers, and team comes from working at the higher levels. After all, work is not a nasty word.

After reading the last few messages, one of our subscribers sent an e-mail telling me I wouldn't have to work at all if I joined his company. That is one of the major flaws of introducing people to direct sales. As recruiters, we tell them "it's so easy, you really don't have to work at it." But that's not true! Building a solid business does take WORK…and lots of it! Remember, the leaders at the top didn't fall there. Yet, when an opportunity is presented, we often say, "Oh, it's so easy, people will flock to you!" Maybe they will after you've put in a whole lot of work!

Use these five levels as you work with your team, customers, and family. You know a host who is so excited about what you'll be teaching at her show doesn't cancel. Kids who love their families stay close. And customers who love you and your service–not just because they get gifts and recognition–will be your customers, hosts, and maybe even team members for a very long time!

Have you discovered the word to help you remember these levels? Let's do a countdown and a recap:

L: Love
E: Expectations
M: Monetary rewards
O: Others' opinions
N: Negative results if work isn't completed.

Put together they spell L E M O N! And when you do the *TWIST*…you'll get Lemon Aid, resulting in Sweet Successes and Juicy Profits!

Chapter Sixteen: The Do Not Call List

Have You Been using The Do Not Call List?

For those Lemon Aid subscribers in the United States, the Federal Communications Commission has developed a National Do Not Call register. If you don't want to receive calls from Telemarketers, you can put your name and number on the list. Conversely, if you are a sales person in any way–not just a paid-per-hour obnoxious telephone solicitor–you are considered a telemarketer and could be fined if you call those people on this list.

Guess what? Most direct sales professionals have been working with this Do Not Call list as long as they have been in the business. Many believe that their friends, family, and customers do not want them to call...so they don't.

Have you been using a "Do Not Call List" in your business? You have if...

• You don't regularly contact customers to check up on the products/services they purchased from you
• You believe you are intruding in their lives when you make a call
• You don't connect with customers on a regular basis to let them know you're still in business and are available to service them
• You assume your customers will call you when they need more of what you offer, so you don't call them
• You don't return phone calls from customers or vendors
• You don't follow through on calling customers when they've requested a call
• You think customer service is like a chess game. If they don't call you after you've left a message, you don't call them back because it's "their" turn
• You act like it's against the law to make business calls
• You experience any kind of Phone Phobia.™

Another interesting phenomenon I've observed, as well as participated in, is we don't appreciate something until we don't have it anymore, and the more we can't have something, the more we want it! Such is the case with this national list.

This is the first time in history that we as consumers have such power over our phones. But as salespeople, our liberty is now limited. Is that going to stop your progress? I hope not.

If you've been a subscriber, you probably know that while I was a leader in a major direct sales company, I moved often. Our family would land in a new area where I knew no one. I had to develop creative ways to meet new customers. One way was to do cold calls on the phone. I'd just begin calling people out of the phone book. Most said no. That's okay. I only needed one or two bookings and then I'd build from there, which is exactly what I did.

When I present these ideas at Lemon Aid Learning Adventures or in my book (*Lead Alphabet*, pages 101-103) I often get the response, "I could never do that!" Well, now, guess what, unless you have purchased the list of numbers on the Do Not Call list, it's against the law to make those calls. (Remember: the entire country is not on this list. You can purchase a list of numbers not to call and then call everybody else. I found the best info at this address: www.ftc.gov/bcp/conline/pubs/alerts/dncbizalrt.htm. You'll find you can get your area code for no cost, or just go to telemarketing.notcall.gov for information.)

Perhaps you haven't appreciated the liberty of picking up the phone book and calling people at random. Maybe you were scared that someone would hang up on you or tell you "no" or even "No, thank you." I can promise I am still alive today, and I have no bruises from people rejecting my invitation. On the other hand, many, many, people's lives were influenced for the better because they not only did business with me, but also began their own profit-making endeavors.

I did not make the calls, nor do I teach making calls, as some telemarketers do: overbearing, boring, uninterested in what you're saying, pushy, obnoxious, doesn't know what the word "no" means. None of us likes that! That's why I never considered myself a "telemarketer." I was always friendly, to the point, considerate of the person's time and response. I didn't try to talk them into doing something they didn't want to do; I was simply looking for "thirsty" people. Unfortunately the actions of many have hindered the work of a few.

If you were one of those who wouldn't do cold calls, the Do Not Call List will have little, if any, impact on your business because you've already been living the law. If you were diligent at meeting folks over the phone, lucky for you…as well as for those people you serviced.

Now we need to do some creative connecting with customers and future customers to demonstrate we are service people.

TWISTS on the Do Not Call List for Party Plan People
As Direct Sales professionals, we certainly have a one up on most sales people when it comes to doing a *TWIST* on the National Do Not Call List. Outside of the Direct Sales industry, most sales people only have the option to work with clients in one-on-one presentations. We have the option, responsibility, and opportunity to hold home demonstrations where we can service people in a fun group setting.

In a recent article, I read that companies are sending their reps out on the streets and off the phones to meet people to skirt the Do Not Call List. I love going to a neighborhood and meeting new people. Many of you are not comfortable with that–even though I have to tell you it's the fastest and easiest way to get bookings (See *Where to Find Customers when you Run out of Family and Friends*, pages 28-30 for tips on this). Most sales people have to scramble for referrals. We honor hosts who introduce us to their friends who then become our next hosts. Holding a consistent schedule of home parties will eliminate the need to ever make cold calls. Thus eliminating fears about calling people who might be registered on the Do Not Call List.

Here are some hints specific to party plan people allowing you to stay within the guidelines of the Do Not Call List while continuing to build your business.

Always get a list of the invitees with their names, phones, and addresses from your host. This list is valuable to both you and the host for many, many reasons (see *Presentations for Profits pages,* 6-8). After the party I'd call those on the list who did not attend to see if they want to order or book. If any of those people are on the "List" you could be breaking the law. So, do the *TWIST*: Offer to make the reminder calls on her behalf so you're meeting– and impressing–guests even *before the demonstration.*

On this quick call, (make it short and sweet for both you and the invitees), you can discover if she has any items she wants you to bring to demonstrate. If she has special requests, you can discover them and give suggestions. For example, if your product is home décor, and she is looking for some accent pieces, have her bring a pillow, a swatch of wallpaper, or a paint chip to the party to coordinate colors. Most people don't think of doing this until they get to the party. This service moves the decision along and gets the right product to the customer faster.

People are gracious when you personally call to remind them. If they cannot attend, they'll usually say, "I do want to order..." At that point, you can take their order...or, get ready for a *TWIST*...invite her to schedule her own show! What a concept...bookings before the party! Honestly, when you *invite*, not pressure, she might agree. I'll admit most kindly decline. You don't need everyone to say "yes." One or two extra bookings like this every month will make a major difference in the number of people you can service.

At your parties be very upfront with customers. Let guests know your primary responsibility is to service their needs. One way you do this is to keep in touch with them via phone, mail, or e-mail, which is why you ask for that information. If they don't want to be contacted, they can simply write, "do not contact" on their order form and assure them they'll get a call from you only if you have a question or problem with their order.

To date, no one has written this. I believe it's because they can feel that I'm not going to harass them. This technique also conveys that you only want to keep in touch with those who want the extra service. You're not desperate for business; rather you're in demand because you are focused on them–not you. This open attitude also helps your business because you're not wasting time calling people who are not "thirsty."

Don't Hang Up on the Do Not Call List—For Direct Sales

What are your feelings on the National Do Not Call List? Mine are mixed. Part of me doesn't mind a phone call once in a while with an offer that I would not know about otherwise. I've actually made some good business choices because someone called me.

On the other hand, sales calls can be an interruption to my life–but I have plenty of other interruptions that yell more loudly than a phone ring. And, I do understand the plight of the elderly, like my father-in-law who suffers from memory loss. When salespeople call, he gets confused and sometimes agrees to offers he doesn't understand. So, this list can be like anything else in life–both good and bad.

So, while I might be frustrated that I don't have the liberty to pick up the phone book and personally contact anyone I want, the Do Not Call List might actually benefit the Direct Sales industry.

First of all, I haven't registered my home phone number on the list, because I've actually done some great recruiting after listening to a telemarketer's message. (See *Where to Find Customers when you run out of Family and Friends*, page 104 for this approach). I've also learned things to say and not say from being the prospect on someone else's calls. So, I'll continue to listen and learn (and maybe share the news about Direct Selling) from these calls—you can too!

Second, the wording on "The List" is for people soliciting sales. Gosh, what if you randomly called people asking if they wanted to make–not spend–money? You're not selling anything this way. I remember calling out of the phone book when I was in a new area and wanted to build my team. I used these words: Jennifer! Christie calling from _____ (your company). I'm adding new Consultants to my team. Do you want more information?" Obviously I got many "no's" but a few yeses. I only needed a few.

Third, one of the biggest "Sour Situations" for the Telemarketing industry with the list is the workforce will be cut back substantially–up to 2 million jobs. According to *USA Today*, the following groups of individuals who are employed with Telemarketing firms might have a tough time finding other jobs: Workers in rural communities (60% of the Telemarketing workforce); recently on public assistance/welfare (30%); full-time students (26%); single mothers (26%) and partially or fully handicapped (5%).

Just think of this scenario: We have possibly two million people who know how to use the phone to gather business, and they are looking for work! One of the ways a person in the Direct Sales industry builds a business is by using the telephone. Let's put two million and two (you and your company) together, and that makes for a lot of recruits! Okay, maybe all two million won't want to have their own business. What if only 10 percent–or even 1 percent–or even one or two of these people you introduce to your business are able to experience true freedom where they'd not have to worry about having their jobs gone due to legislation? Then I'd say the Do Not Call List is a blessing in disguise for many people, specifically those in the groups mentioned above.

As you huddle with your hosts, ask them to invite everyone they know who has or has had a telemarketing job. Just think, they've already overcome one of the biggest hurdles we all face as we begin a new business–getting on the phone!

Lastly, the other great lesson we are forced (sometimes that's the only way I finally "get it") to learn with the implementation of the Do Not Call List is to stay connected with customers. If a person is on "the list" you can legally contact her up to 18 months after her last order with you. That's a long time to wait! I'm confident most of you communicate with your clientele much more frequently. And I also know that my Lemon Aid Learners call to service as well as sell. And, that if a customer asks not to be contacted the request is respectfully honored.

We'll often have "Sour Situations" in our lives and business. The key is to do the *TWIST* and focus on what we can do—rather than what we can't. In this respect, we're sure to have many Sweet Successes and Juicy Profits we'd never have otherwise. I can't think of a better industry to be involved in as we see these changes come into our lives.

Chapter Seventeen: Prescriptions for Phone Phobia

What's Lurking in Your Home Office?

WARNING! A creature is lurking in your house/office. See if you can guess what it is:

• It doesn't weigh very much; maybe 2 pounds

• Sometimes you can carry it with you, other times it is hanging out on the wall...or even your desk...oh no!

• This creature makes funny sounds, but when you hear the sounds you're not usually afraid, in fact sometimes you ENJOY the sound

• Some people would rather wash dishes, scrub floors, or even fold laundry to avoid this creature

• Can you believe you PAY to have this creature around your home/office, but you don't have to feed it

• If used correctly, it can actually help FEED you, your family, and your business

• This creature has given some people a disease; however, it is not terminal, it can be "turnable" if you do the *TWIST*...

The disease is PHONE PHOBIA...afraid of picking up the ? Have you guessed it? The answer is the PHONE! Many of you have expressed a real fear about picking up the phone and making calls to potential customers/hosts/recruits. How do you *TWIST* this FEARFUL FOE(ne)into a FAITHFUL FRIEND? The same way you conquer any fears, by facing them! The phone will be in your home even if you never call anyone. It will even ring once in a great while and people on the other end might even be calling to place an order, schedule a demonstration, or to join your team. If this creature is so wonderful when receiving INBOUND calls, why are we so fearful in making OUTBOUND calls? I believe we're fearful because of what's on the other end...

But some people believe the person called will be some sort of a scary spook who will haunt them forever. I have ideas for making calls...many are written in the Lemon Aid Lead and Deed Alphabet books and I've posted some to this list. But the best answer I have is to just DO IT! Most people, even if they don't want your product/service won't say BOO... the scariest thing they'll say is NO! After all, the person on the other end could be your next HOST!

Have a Passion for Your Business

Don't even think of picking up the phone–either incoming or outgoing calls–unless you have a PASSION for yourself and for your business. This passion cannot be disguised like someone in a costume; people will see right through you. Furthermore, they'll feel your hesitation and unbelief. You gotta have that passion in a passionate way.

Here's an illustration: I am really phobic about FIRE. I don't think any of us would want to be caught in a burning building. But what if you saw a building burning? What would you do? Would you hesitate and think, "I'll call later, it will probably burn out–after all the firefighters might be in the middle of dinner; I really don't want to bother them."
What if you did get the courage to tell the fire department this important news? What would you say when you dialed 9 1 1? Would these be your words: "Hi..uh..uh..oh... how are you doing? Excuse me, I really hate to bother anyone over at the station. I think I see a burning building across the street; it does smell kind of smokey. You wouldn't want to bring your big red fire trucks down to put out the fire, would you?"

WHAT IS WRONG WITH THIS? If I saw a fire, I'd run to the phone...dial 9-1-1, and with all the passion and persuasion, I'd say "FIRE! FIRE! 125 Main Street! Help! Hurry!"
In other words, I want to get my point across as soon as possible with all the passion I had.

Now, how can this be *TWISTED* to picking up the phone? Have a passion for what you are calling about! If you don't believe your message, don't call. If you do...if you KNOW what you're going to share will have a positive impact on a person's life, home, needs, wants, then get those fingers punching those phone numbers with a BURNING PASSION–don't let anything put that passion out!

What Passionate message can you send to people over the phone this week?

Phone Phobias, Two

Our last message was on having PASSION before you pick up the phone. Not only do you want to renew that passion each time before you dial, you also want to **identify your phone phear**. Most consultants will say the biggest phear is that people will say "no." That's only one of the phears. Here are some others that contribute to PhonePhobia:

You're phearful that:

• It won't be a good time for the prospect. We "think" she might be preparing dinner, watching her favorite TV show, reading her kids a story, or just sitting down to read the paper. In other words, **the real phear is that we will become an intrusion in her life rather than an inspiration**. Don't think...just dial!

- It's been so long since you talked to her your phear is that **she might not remember you**. This could be true, but when you politely remind her ("I met you at Jennifer's show last year"), she'll make the connection.

- You've waited so long to follow through since you met her at the fair, home expo, etc. **The phear is that she'll think you're a slacker for not getting back to her sooner.** So? Have you heard of "better late than never?" In fact, maybe it is better that you're later. Maybe now her appetite is really hungering for what you have to offer. Maybe earlier would not have been better. Either way, you'll never know till you call.

- Your potential customer/hostess/recruit has joined/booked with another consultant or with a competing company. Here is where your **phear turns to humility when you realize she could have been with you had you picked up the phone earlier**. In this case, better early than later. This is one of the times I hope "phear motivation" kicks in and that you have a phone frenzy and call everyone on your list to be sure this doesn't happen again. Don't beat yourself up if you find that her mom, best friend or someone else close to her is her sponsor or consultant. In this case, the timing of your call probably would not have made any difference. In any case, always wish her the best.

- The person might not take you seriously or even laugh or mock you. This happens most often with close friends and families. They question your association with your company ("You're still selling that stuff?"). The real phear is questioning yourself if you've done/are doing the right thing. This is where passion can overcome rejection (that's why you've got to be PASSIONATE first!). You have to know in advance that you have made the right decision—you've got to have that 9-1-1 PASSION and then PROVE 'EM WRONG. Revenge can be sweet when, in the future, they phone you to book a demonstration because they've heard from so many people how great you are…it will happen!

- The prospect might just say YES. This, believe it or not, is a PHEAR of many people. If the person says YES to wanting more information, are you prepared to visit with her or send her what she wants? If she says YES to scheduling a demonstration, are you prepared with the dates that are best for you, or will you have to call her back after you've had a chance to check your calendar. What if she says YES to joining your team. Now you have another responsibility: to teach her how to start a business. Have you prepared time for this in your schedule? **If you are not prepared, you will phear**…

- The person might say NO…Remember, "no" doesn't usually mean "never." Ask her if she wants you to call her another time. If she says "no" again, it's okay. Phoning is not a "no" game, it's a nos. (numbers) game. The more calls, the more no's, the more no's, the more yeses will eventually come. **No's aren't really a phear, they're only the road to the yeses**.

What other phears haunt you before you pick up the phone? When you know your phear, do the *TWIST* and discover what the phear really is. Then, let your passion rule and your fingers dial!

Phone Phobia, Three

One of our phobias for not calling and contacting people is that we're *worried about what they're going to think*:

• All she cares about is building her business
• Why is she involved in that company?
• Is she desperate for cash?
• Is she crazy?
• Why doesn't she get a "real job?"

But, why do we care if people think this? Actually, most people don't think any of those statements. If they don't want to take advantage of your product/service/offer, they'll simply say "no." They normally don't care about you. Yes…I said, they normally don't care about you and what you're involved in.

Do you remember the day before the biggest dance of the year? You know the day—the day you had the biggest pimple you've ever had on your face. You just knew "everybody was going to notice." You spent all this time putting creams and concoctions on the blemish and were self-conscious about it the entire evening. At the end of the evening, I bet no one even noticed your "sour situation." And you know why they didn't notice? Because they were too concerned about the blemishes on their own faces or the nick in their nail polish or a scuff on their shoes. See…most of us are too self-absorbed to think about what someone else is really doing. This is human nature.

Last week, Heather Mills McCartney—newly wed bride of the former Beatle—was a guest on Larry King Live. She is an *amazing* woman. Larry King asked where she and Paul were on September 11, 2001. They were on a plane waiting to take off from JFK airport in New York. Heather said she suggested that Paul do a benefit concert to aid the victims. You know what he, a member of one of the most-recognized musical groups ever, said? He was worried that people would think he would be doing it solely to promote his new album! Imagine that! Paul McCartney was worried what other people would think! He did, however, hold the concert and raised millions of dollars. Not many thought what he thought they'd think. And so what if someone thought he was being self-promoting? Thousands of people benefited from his generosity. And, in the process, many probably purchased his new album. So more than one person benefited. Is that a problem?

Are we thinking that when we offer our product/service to people that we're the only one who profits? Yes, we make money when someone buys from us. We add volume to our team, and we might even qualify for a car or a trip or other gifts! But, aren't the customers also winners? Of course! And if you didn't make that contact, wouldn't everyone be losers? Maybe. Yes, you'd lose out on a sale and profit and they'd lose out on what you offered. However, someone else can contact them, or maybe they'll go to the mall. The real loser here would just be the person with the phobia. When we know that what we offer people is advantageous to them, why are we so timid to let them know?

We're not in an athletic game where we have a winner and a loser. We're not in a duel with our customers; we're in a duet. All of us are winners when we overcome the phobia of "What are people going to think?" I believe people will think, and say, "Thank you for servicing me and keeping in touch!"

After all, our call is to offer them TREATS, never tricks! Who wouldn't open their door, or ears to this? All you need to do is open your mouth!

Phone Phobia, Four—Partnering so Your Phobia will Depart

I'm going to share one of the easiest ways to have your phone phobia depart your life. Choose a partner! This is a really fun, effective exercise that will help two–not just you! You can't choose just anyone. You must choose someone who, like you, is serious (not just kidding) about building a business. Next, you and this person must commit (not just kid) to connect every day for the next week for just ten minutes a day. No excuses will be allowed. The time of day doesn't have to be the same every day, but you must have the ten-minute segments scheduled for the entire week. Remember: NO EXCUSES for missing out on the appointment.

You're going to be Partner A (for Awesome). Your friend is Partner G (for Great). The first day you call Partner G and you both pretend she's a potential customer/host/recruit. She plays the part. In other words, she acts like a contact does. She gives reasons why she can't do business with you, never to call again, or she might even say "yes", and so forth. Here's an example:

A: "Great, this is Awesome calling from _____" (your company name and then you proceed with what you want to talk with her about)
G: Will respond just as a customer would. Don't be "easy" on A just because you're practicing. Instead, use scenarios that you've heard from your own customers/contacts.

This practicing with your partner will not create perfection. It will help you with the words to say. You can go through at least five scenarios during this time. The next day "G" makes the phone call to "A" who is the customer.

If you both do this faithfully for an entire week, your confidence in calling will increase. Another form of phobia is we're not sure what to say (I've never been much for verbatim scripts). This practice will put the words in your mouth as you use wisdom in your responses.

Partnering will put out your phobias. Practice will not make perfect...it will make profits. The more you practice the more you profit the more your phobias will depart!

Pre Phoning to Eliminate Phone Phobia

Are you a promise keeper? I trust so. You wouldn't commit to doing a task for a customer (or anyone else) and then not do it. Overcoming Phone Phobia is simply keeping your promise to communicate with your customers, hosts, and other prospects. A *TWIST* on picking up the phone or sending literature is *layering* your marketing communications with both modes as you keep your promise.

You might follow the example of many Party Plan professionals and send your newest catalogs, mini catalogs, or flyers as soon as they are released to those in your database. Several companies even offer a service where they do the mailings to the names you provide–I highly recommend participating in these programs.

As a customer, I love knowing what's new when I receive these. I notice that most come with a note *for me to call* my consultant so I can order or schedule a demonstration. I know as your customers thumb through your literature, they'll mentally make notes of what they want and maybe even consider booking with you.

Here are the important questions: Do they call you or visit your website? Are you seeing a return on the investment you've made in postage and materials with increased sales and bookings? Now is time to follow through and pick up the phone. This is *layered* marketing communications.

And, now you have a great reason to call. First, you want to be sure the package was received. Next, you want to discover if the person is eager to take advantage of the host/customer offers in the literature. If she has a couple of minutes to chat, point out some of the items you feel she'd especially want. What a service! As much as I love my Land's End® and assorted other catalogs, I've never had one of their people call to see if I got the catalog and take me on a "page tour." My sister and I were just talking the other day about how we love to order from catalogs, but we drag our feet thinking we'll wait until we have a lot of time to sit down and "shop." That time rarely comes! On the other hand, if someone called us, we'd take action.

When you make this phone call, you can also find out if she chooses not to receive your information. Maybe her co-worker just joined your company (you hadn't met the co-worker, so don't feel bad that she's not on your team) and your customer wants to support her. Or, she might not want any more of your product. Or she is moving to Siberia. Or, or, or… In other words this contact helps you to "dust your database!"

When you participate in mass mailings, schedule time for telephoning about two weeks after the mail has arrived to call each person.

What if you only have two new catalogs a year? Should you continue to contact people? Yes, yes, yes! If you have the *Sweet Holiday Success* CD, listen to the segment on "Creating a Business Horn of Plenty" (Track 11) and use the cards in the FREE bonus booklet to pre-phone any time of year. For example, if you've heard through the grapevine that one of your customers is having a difficult time right now because her husband is serving in Iraq, send her the postcard that says, "When Life gives you Lemons, schedule a (fill in the blank part with your company and demonstration)". On the card, note that you'll call her next to the words "Call Me." What a concept! Announcing that you'll make the connection rather than asking her to take the next step!

Here's another idea for Pre Phoning: With your computer, create a postcard (I like postcards because the prospect doesn't have to open anything to get your message) that reads: What is special about the following dates?

Now, list your next three available dates for bookings, but don't explain anything else. On the bottom on the card, write: "I'll call you soon with the answer." When you call her, she's probably very curious. You can disclose the mystery and obtain a new booking!

Your strategy for Pre Phoning should be to send out only as many cards as you know you can follow up on. For example, send out ten cards a week, and make the phone calls for those the following week. Send ten more, call the next week, and so on. This turns out to be more effective than sending out hundreds at a time where you're playing the lottery hoping you'll get one percent of the people responding. By the way, one percent response is considered a great return on a direct mail piece. When you layer it with a phone call, the results will multiply dramatically.

And, in the process…you're Phone Phobias will begin to disappear!

Post Phoning to Overcome Phone Phobia
Last week, I shared ideas about how to link up with customers and prospects before you pick up the phone. This week the subject is what to do after you make calls: Post Phoning–and I don't mean to procrastinate making the calls, but to be proactive after you've dialed.

When you make phone calls to increase your business, you typically get one of these responses:

- No–I don't want to take advantage of what you're offering.
- Not Now–but you can call me again
- Not for me–but here is a name of someone else to call
- Need more information–send me something or schedule an appointment to meet
- Nice !! I'm ready to do business with you

In each instance, plans for post-phoning–what to do after a call–need to be in place. Here's what I suggest for each scenario:

No–I don't want to take advantage of what you're offering

Put this person's name in a file of "not to call" people. Even if they ask not to be contacted again, I cannot bring myself to throwing a name and phone number out. I honor their request by not calling and indicate so in my records. However, I can send them a Thank You for visiting with me on the phone note. That's it. A note that says, "Thanks for visiting me. I know what I have to offer is not what you're looking for right now. If you know someone else wanting to replace their carpets [you insert what product or service you offer], thanks for referring them to me. Here's my number for your reference."

Not Now–but you can call me again

These are your future business contacts. The first thing I ask is "When do you want me to call you next?" Let them tell you. Many times it is sooner than you think. Now, I put this information in my Business Bank (read more about this in the *Deed Alphabet: The Deeds you Need to Convert Leads to Committed Customers*, pages 18-20). Most of the time when someone says, "Not now," she has a reason. Refer to this in your Post Phone communication:

Send a quick postcard: "Jane! Enjoyed visiting with you today. I promise to call you at the beginning of February to schedule your _____ show/class/party. In the meantime, have a BLAST on your January cruise. If you need any lotion or sunscreen [or whatever your product is appropriate to her reason for not taking action is] before you go, I can service you quickly."

Another example, I started having my carpets cleaned by a company who did cold calling from the phone book. I have been impressed that Bob, the telemarketer, always calls back when I ask, and have been pleased with their carpet care. The last few times Bob called, my reason to not have my carpets cleaned is I'm replacing some of my carpet with tile. When that's finished, I want the remaining carpets in my house cleaned so I'll have clean floors everywhere.

For Post Phone service, he could write me a note stating: "Good luck getting your tile installed; I'll call you in January as you've requested to schedule your carpet cleaning. For your information, we also have a tile cleaning service to keep your new tiles maintained."

Not for me, but here is the name of someone you should call
The residual result from consistent calling is you'll get referrals from your customers. If your customer has loved the new frying pan she purchased from you, but doesn't need any of your products, she might say, "I don't need anything, but my mom is dying to get her own pan after using mine. Can you call her?"

After contacting your customer's referral, call the first customer back to thank her. Even better, send her a thank you note–even if the referral doesn't end up purchasing anything from you.

Need more information–send me something or schedule an appointment to meet
As you advertise your business through personal phone calls, a prospect's curiosity is piqued…but she may not be fully convinced. Your post phoning activity here is to give her pertinent information to aid in making her decision. This could be inviting her to visit your website or by sending her a catalog, a flyer, or a sample.

Be cautious here. Some consultants (I did it all the time) immediately ask (probably because it's a quick and painless way to get off the call), "Do you want me to send you a catalog?" In an effort to get you off the phone, many reply in the affirmative. So, offer this only if you feel like her curiosity has now developed into true interest.

Now…here's the most important way to use this Post Phoning idea: "I'll put a catalog in the mail today, Wednesday. You'll have it within seven days. Can we set up a phone appointment right now so we can go a 'catalog tour?' I have next Wednesday at this same time–10:00 a.m., does that work for you? Of course, you're welcome to call me before that if you're too excited to wait!" If she's not willing to set up another call, her interest level might not be sufficient to send a catalog; you decide.

If the prospect lives near you, I suggest scheduling a face-to-face appointment. This is the richest form of communication, and booking, selling, and recruiting is much more effective for all parties involved.

Setting up an appointment as part of Post Phoning is conveying to your prospect that you're interested in servicing her, not just blowing her off by sticking something in the mail. Remember, your goal is to make a profit–for yourself, not the postal service.

Nice! I'm ready to do business with you
Be prepared for YESES ! Have your calendar handy with the dates you have available for

booking, Host Huddling, interviews, or whatever activity is next. These are the ultimate Post Phoning Activities.

To further reinforce Post Phoning when a customer takes action, always send a Thank You note–not an E-mail, but a real live handwritten note of sincere appreciation. When you do this, people will look forward to more and more calls from you. As they anticipate your calls, your Phone Phobia diminishes!

Calling Plans to Eliminate Phone Phobia

Every phone supplier of both landline phones and cellular phones offers a myriad of phone calling plans; they can be very confusing! As a user you get mixed up as to what time of day you can phone at reduced rates, where can you call and not be charged long distance and roaming fees, when is your billing cycle that begins your monthly minutes, can your minutes be rolled over to next month? Confusing? Confusing! Some plans have benefits that others don't; you'd like to mix and match them, but that's not an option, as you have to choose just one company with one plan.

While you can't change the Calling Plans of phone companies, you can create your own Calling Plan, which will eliminate your personal Phone Phobias and increase your income. Let me share the Calling Plans I've used in my business. Which do you want to subscribe to?

The first calling plan I used was the **Thinking About It Plan**. You might assume this means my customers told me they were "thinking about it" when I offered them my product or service. Actually, they never had an opportunity to "think about it" because I rarely connected with them because instead of dialing, I was just "thinking about calling." Usually I'd be thinking they'd say no, not have time to talk, not be home, not be needing my information, and so on. I did a lot of thinking for my customers! Since I spent so much time "thinking about" calling, I felt like I had worked all day long without any results! When, in fact, I made very few calls.

For a long time I had the **Desperate Calling Plan**. I'd just get on the phone when I was low on business–which is the worse time to make calls because I conveyed a depressed attitude. I don't suggest signing up for this plan; it's very emotionally expensive! Have you heard the suggestion that the best time to look for a new job is when you're employed? That's because if a new company doesn't hire you, you're still employed. The same concept holds true for connecting with customers. You get the best results when you're actually too busy for more business!

Then I developed the **Perfect Calling Plan**. Meaning, I made calls only when I felt like everything was perfect: my environment, my time, my calendar, and my prospects' clocks. This rarely worked as I never found the perfect time, place or person to call.

After attending a seminar on phone calling, I joined the **Confusing Calling Plan**. The instructor taught that every time I made a call, I scored a point! If I actually talked to someone, I added two points. If the prospect said, "I want more information," I got to add five points. If they said, "yes" to my offer, I got ten points, or was it fifteen? If someone was rude and hung up, I scored a whopping fifty points—I suppose this was to award perseverance.

I had a lot of fun tallying up the points for the first few calls. Then, I couldn't remember if a "Call me another time" response was worth five or ten points. How many points did I give myself if I left a voice mail? I couldn't remember. Pretty soon, my brain was confused and I couldn't remember why I was calling people in the first place. Ah...then I remembered my goal wasn't to add points, it was to add customers! I was too focused on myself. Yes, I was punching a lot of number keys–on my calculator, not my phone! The surprise was, no one was ever rude or hung up! So much for the fifty-point bonus!

Another Calling Plan was the **Hit or Miss Plan,** meaning I'd miss the prospect and get voice mail or I'd want to hit them (figuratively, of course) when they replied, "I'm not interested." I felt like I was making a lot of calls with no progress until I started to keep track of my calls and responses. Again, I was amazed to find I really hadn't made many calls; I just felt I had.

Finally, I created the **Committed, Consistent Calling Plan**, which has built my businesses for years and years. It's very simple and customer focused. This plan began when I made a commitment to increase my sales. I calculated I only needed to make forty calls a week to have a significant impact on my business. That double-digit number might seem overwhelming to you. However, I broke it down into smaller bites so that I was contacting just eight people a day. These weren't only brand-new leads, they were also persons who I had done business with in the past and wanted to service better.

The best way to see results is by *easily tracking* them, so I created a simple tracking system: a spiral-bound notebook. A hard copy, rather than electronic data, was preferable to me because of its portability and tangibility. This notebook stared at me several times a day and was easy to pack if I knew I had the time and place to make phone calls while I was in between appointments or had some waiting time. At the beginning of each week, I numbered the lines on two or three pages from 1-40. Every eighth line (8, 16, 24, 32, 40) had a distinct mark, usually a yellow highlighter, run across it to represent my daily calls.

Some days I only had an opportunity to make three or four contacts. The next day, I knew I needed to make up the other three or four. I soon learned that playing "catch up" wasn't fun! Some days, I did extra calls–maybe ten or twelve–so I was ahead of my goal. This visual boosted my discipline. I might have had only three minutes till I had to leave for an appointment, and I'd see the notebook. So I'd hurry and dial and connect with a customer.

Obviously not everyone took me up on my offer to do business at that time. Many people asked me to call back, and I built up a substantial Business Bank. That simple, daily habit created an increase of over 25% in my sales from the previous year. That ain't too shabby!

Your business might be brand new, with just a few customers. Your Calling Plan will need to include more minutes each month–maybe even some cold calling. However most people do just the opposite. The approach is, "I can't make many calls because I don't now many people." Actually, you probably know more *thirsty* people than you think. Start dialing.

As your business grows, keep using the Committed, Consistent Calling Plan. You might not call as many people in a day as you did when you were at the "brand new" stage. However, this plan will become your maintenance plan so your business never gets sick due to lack of customers.

Which plan will you use?

Five Fun-Der-Ful ways to Communicate When the Phone is not the Answer

Sometimes a phone isn't the best way to bommunicate. As much as I am a strong advocate for using the phone as a business and relationship-building tool, you'll have situations where the phone may not be the best mode of communicating with a customer, host, or recruit.

In my book, *Hanging up on your Phone Phobias*, you'll read **50 Fun-der-ful Ideas to use when the phone is not the answer**, including how to put together a Success Kit for new recruits. If you've attended my Lemon Aid for Leaders class, you might have seen this; now you'll have it in print.

Here are Five Fun-der-Ful Ways specific to the Party Plan industry (these are not in the book) to connect with hosts, customers, or team members as well as the appropriate situations for using the ideas.

1. Delay in closing a party

When a host is not getting all her orders and payments to you to close out her party, or returning your phone calls, send her a *sheet of wrapping paper*. On the back of it, write:

"Let's wrap up your party so you can get all your gifts. Please call me at ___ or send the orders and payments to me at _____ When I have the orders by _____, you can expect your packages of products to arrive by _____. You'll have lots of reasons to celebrate!"

Here's a *TWIST*: Send the wrapping paper before the party to remind host when to have all orders and payments to you. Use the words: "Let's wrap up your orders on the evening of your party so you can..."

2. Customer Service issue where you haven't serviced the customer as you know you should

Send a *small bouncy ball* with a note saying, "You probably feel like you've been bounced around because I haven't _____. I apologize and assure you that I'm back on the ball and will take care of the situation so I can be part of your winner's circle."

3. Pre-phone call

Send your newest catalog or mailer along with a *toy ring* (buy at the novelty shops or dollar stores) Include a note: "I'll be giving you a ring next week to assist you in ordering, booking a class, or joining our team."

4. Recruiting idea

For a mom of young children who you know wants to get out of the house, but has reservations about beginning a new business, send an *unused disposable diaper*:

"Are you're feeling stinky about life and are looking for a change so you can still be #1 Mom? Let's get together and "wipe" down the details." Hey, if she doesn't take you up on your offer, she'll remember you each time she changes a diaper–and now she even has an extra diaper!

I personally love this idea because I was this young mom who loved my son and was looking for a little extra in my life. If someone sent me this, I'd have signed up right away...after I quit laughing!

5. To remind host to return her guest list and other pre-party challenges

Send a decorated paper bag (order fun stamps and stickers from our Direct Sales friends in those companies) or purchase from our Party Plan friends who sell decorative bags. On the outside, neatly tape a message: "A successful party will be in the bag when you…"

• Return your guest list to me
• Call and remind your guests.
• Have $_____ orders paid in advance
• Have one booking before I arrive

Each of the above suggestions can be on separate pieces of paper she'll find in the bag.

Okay, my ideas are still flowing, so I'll share a sixth idea with you:

6. Team Motivation

Send a toy yo-yo (go to the "Dollar" store) with the following message:
You won't meet your go-goals if your party schedule is like a yo-yo–sometimes up and sometimes down. It's up to you-you to get go-going

Chapter Eighteen: Presentations for Profit

Your Guest Book

When you go to a wedding reception, do you recall how you sign the Guest Book? The Bride and Groom want to have a permanent record of who joined their celebration. Your home party is also a celebration that you'll want a permanent record of who was in attendance. Here's how and why I use this great tool:

After everyone has been seated, and I'm just about to begin my demonstration, I invite my guests to "autograph" my Guest Book (sounds better than "sign"). I explain, just as I did in the previous paragraph, that I want to remember who joined us tonight. This Guest Book is simply a sheet of paper where each guest lists her name, phone, and address. [You'll find a sample that you can photocopy and use at your shows in the appendix of the *Presentations for Profit$* book along with *TWISTS* in putting your Guest Book together.]

Why do you really need this information? Have you ever had a guest leave before placing her order with the words, "I'll call you later with my order?" And does she? Not always. And why doesn't she? Because she's busy and placing the order is not always on her list of priorities. After time goes by, she figures it might be too late and decides she'll order next time.

So, why not do the *TWIST* and call her? If you received a Guest List from your hostess, you can get her name from that. Oh, you don't get Guest Lists? (Read pages 1-19 of the book and you'll want to!) That's okay, her name and phone number are on the order form... which she took with her! But wait! You do have her information on your Guest Book! So, pick up that phone and give her a call.

Think of all the times you have customers who combine their orders to save on the shipping and handling. If you rely solely on the order forms to gather guests' names and phone numbers, then you only have one of the two (or sometimes more) guests. With a Guest Book, you have everyone's!

And, have you ever had a guest who you really wanted to interview for your business, but she either left early or didn't order and you don't have her name and phone number? Or, maybe you do get a Guest List from your hostess. However, she invited some people who weren't on the list and some people brought friends, and they didn't all place orders? In this case, you don't have all the names and phone numbers you need. You will with a Guest Book!

In all the years I used a Guest Book, I only had one person question the reason for the book. I can see her now. She questioned my motive, "By signing this, am I signing up to do a party?" "Oh, no," I teasingly assured her, "I only allow people to be hostesses by personal invitation." She gave a slight laugh, autographed the book, and guess who was the first guest to ask me if she could be a hostess?

You might have heard me say before, "Names are worth MILLIONS." This Guest Book will be one very, very, valuable paper with potential for profits!
Some of you use Door Prize Drawing Slips, and might have the information on those. However, not everyone fills those out, and I'm going to share a fun *TWIST* on that item in a future post.

The Guest List, One—What is the number one fear of a potential host?

When I ask that question at Lemon Aid Learning Adventures across the country, I always get the same answer. The biggest fear is that no one will come! It's a common fear because it affects our ego. If we plan for a big event and no one (or only a few come), our feelings are hurt. We think people don't like us. Even though grown up people are grown up, we like to feel important. So this fear, by far, is the reason many people just say "no" to being a host.

So, how do we do the *TWIST*? First, *eliminate the excuse before you encounter it*. When someone uses this excuse as an explanation, simply reply, "I have a list of 40 people who want to attend your presentation." When I used to say this to potential hosts, they looked at me in amazement almost saying, "How do you know my friends?" Before they could verbalize their feelings, I showed them my Top 40 list.

I know what most of you are thinking…you're thinking, "I have a list like that." And you probably do. It's probably just like the ones I see in most Presentation Planning Kits. It lists categories of people. Here's an example of what I've seen for years:

Encourage your host to invite a:
• Teacher
• Video store clerk
• Nurse
• Fireman
• Clerk at store
• Teller at the bank
• Parents of children's friends
• PTA Member
• Co Worker
• Spouse's co-worker

Does this look/sound familiar? These are okay if you want to do an okay business. But if you want to have a business full of Sweet Successes and Juicy Profits, you need to do the *TWIST*!

First, remember the Number One Lemon Aid Law for Locating Leads—found in the book *Where to Find Customers when you run out of Family and Friends*. This law states "Know your Product so you know who your Prospects are." So, what does this have to do with a Top 40 list? Everything.

Examine…not merely look at…EVERY product in your catalog. With each examination ask yourself, "Who needs/wants this product?" Let me illustrate. I have a Longaberger® catalog in front of me. One of their popular baskets is for holding tissues. Everyone who has allergies needs this basket. After all, they sniffle all the time and sneeze once an hour or more! So, on my Top 40 List, I ask my host to invite all persons who suffer with allergies.

Now I'm looking at a catalog from The Angel Company®. Their product is rubber stamps. I see several sets of butterfly stamps. On my Top 40, I ask my host to invite everyone who collects butterflies. Now, this could go more ways than one (which is precisely my point!). Scientists collect butterflies, kids collect butterflies, even my good friend Dotty Winkelman collects items with butterflies on them. As my host reads this, she thinks of several people who would really WANT the product. They now are more interested to come to a presentation because I have something they'll WANT and NEED.

One more company example: My good friend Donita Dahm with Lady Remington Jewelry recently sent me the new catalog. If I were a host, I might be thinking only of friends who wear jewelry, which would limit the people I invite. However, now I have a Top 40 list and it includes:

• Everyone who has a dog.
• All people who love hats.
• Friends who wear fashion scarves.
• Persons with the name "Trish."
• All "Wizard of Oz" fans.

Now, let's examine why these are on my Top 40. One of the pins is a cute puppy. One pin is a fashion hat and another pin is a profile of a woman wearing a large brimmed hat. Several items are scarf clips or scarf tubes. One of the necklaces is named "Trish." And for all Wizard of Oz fans, we would want to buy a pin of the red, glittery shoes that look like Dorothy's red ruby slippers.

Are you doing the *TWIST*? Are you seeing how putting needs/wants of specific people rather than simply general groups will encourage and excite your host? I hope you noticed one more very important way I worded these specific people…I used the plural. Notice the words, "everyone," "all people," "friends," "persons." "all_____". This subconsciously has them thinking of multiple people.

Lastly, here are a few specifics that I put on every Top 40: "The person you scheduled your presentation from." This is the only time I use a singular term. This is also always the first person I list. Most new hosts think that the previous host she scheduled from has received all the products she wants. We know this is rarely, if ever, the case.

Additionally, I do some really fun things when the previous host attends. Other standard suggestions are "Persons with a birthday the month of your presentation." You can recognize these folks. "All persons you know who are experiencing a challenging time." These are the people who really need to get out of the house! And maybe into a new business! "People who play the lottery or enter Sweepstakes." These people like to get something for nothing. They make great hosts!

If your group or company has hired me to do this presentation, you might already have a Top 40 list that I created for you. I hope you're using it. If you don't have one, this is a service I provide when I do company-specific classes.

The Guest List, Two

May I ask a favor of you, my Lemon Aid Learners? For every presentation you have on your calendar as of today, please take two 20-dollar bills, go to the bank and convert them into 40 one-dollar bills. Now, if you have worked with your host and she has developed a strong guest list–including each guest's name, address, and phone number–and given you a copy of this list, you get to invest that money in any way you choose: savings, purchase stocks, etc.

If you have not worked with a host in this regard, and she is simply going to invite the people without this tool, take the 40 one-dollar bills, stand outside on your front porch and toss them to the wind.

I already know none of you would be so foolish as to throw money out your door like that! However, if you are not using a Host Guest List to assist your host and build your business, you are throwing a lot of money out the door and your hosts are not having as successful presentations as they could have.

The benefits to a host when she uses this list are as many–if not more–than the benefits to your business. It's all in the way you present the concept to her, which again will be discussed in subsequent posts.

In addition to the "Top 40" list you have created to give her ideas on whom to invite, give each host an "official list" for her to fill out. This "official list" has room for her to put each guest's name, address, and phone number. Again, the reason for collecting this information will be given as we go along.

Why have an "official guest list?" It keeps your host organized. She has plenty of space to write the info, and when she writes down the names, she is more committed to following through and calling her friends. This also gives her a guide as she makes her calls. Teach her to code with letters:

M: Maybe she'll attend
N: No, she won't be coming; no interest in products or ordering
O: Order because she can't make it
P: Positively will be there!
Q: Quadruple the attendance by bringing friends

Give each host at least two guest lists. If she has more people than will fit on one, she might not keep inviting. Also, in addition to the Top 40 list that you have created, encourage her to have people from at least 7 different zip codes.

The Guest List, Three

Now that your host has an "official guest list" and your own Top 40, she can begin the writing and inviting process. For years, I nearly demanded that the list be returned to me within 24 hours. Then I realized that she might have already scheduled her next 24 hours with other activities and appointments! So, I suggest you ask her, "Will you be able to write your list and invite your guests within the next three days?" Let her lead you as to when this can be completed. This just gives her some breathing room and you're not mad if the list doesn't get to you in the next couple of days. In fact, if she tells you all the activities she has going on in the next couple days, remind her to take the list along so she can invite the people she'll be interacting with. Sometimes she might not think of that.

Even though she has the Top 40 list, sometimes brains still cramp! I remember when my son was getting married and I was creating the guest list for the reception. I sat down to write the list under the friends/neighbors/relatives categories. I had writer's block! But while I was vacuuming the house, or driving my car, I thought of names. Your host is the same way. She might sit down right away and put names on paper, but if you give her a couple of days to have it completed, she'll have a more complete list.

Additionally, because you'll want her to **compose**, **call**, and **code the list**, she needs to have some time to do this. The urgency of having the list back to you also has a great deal to do with how soon the presentation is. Even if it's four to six weeks away, getting it back quickly is a benefit for both you and the host. For you because you know she's committed and for her because she's invited everyone already!

While she's preparing the list and inviting her people, one of the most significant steps to a successful show/party/presentation is to send her a thank you note for scheduling the date with you–send it before the ink is dry on your calendar! Note that I did not say to send a thank you note after she's had a successful event–although you'll do that as well. If you send this attractive, fun, thank you note to her **ASAB** (**A**s **S**oon **A**s **B**ooked), she'll receive it during the time you've asked her to compose the list. This is a subtle reminder and when she is recognized for simply setting a date, she is encouraged to act. For a real *TWIST* on Thank You Notes, read "Fifty Fun-der-ful Ways to Connect wih Prosects and Customers" in my book *Hanging Up on Your Phone Phobias*, pages 129-144.

Snail mail was the only way to get a guest list in the "old days." And it is still effective–along with some other alternatives. Many consultants enclose a self-addressed, stamped envelope to make returning the list a simple step. With today's technology, you can suggest she e-mail or fax the list. This is a bit more difficult if you have the nifty guest lists with duplicate copies. But she'll have her list, you'll have yours, and you'll just need one for mailing labels–which can be easily typed on your computer (more about this with a *TWIST* later on!). I've also had hosts dictate the list to me over the phone. It's more time intensive, but the task was completed.

Within five days of her booking the demonstration, call to see how the guest list is coming if you haven't received it already. This contact is another opportunity to encourage her. If you don't have a list returned within ten days to two weeks, don't be mad...be glad...you have a reason to call her. Very likely you have a host with cold fingers–she quit dialing! Her enthusiasm has waned and she'll be glad to get some encouragement from you. It's amazing what an upbeat call will do for a host. After all, if she called three people and everyone said "no," she's quit calling. She needs you!

If I don't have a list after it was promised, I use the mail system as a scapegoat. "Mary, your guest list hasn't arrived; I'm wondering if my post office has lost it! [My apologies if I've offended any postal workers with that statement!] She'll either give you an excuse or a reason why she hasn't completed it. In rare occasions, she has decided to cancel but didn't want to disappoint you, so she decided she'd wait till the day of the presentation. While I abhorred cancellations, I'd rather know right away so I can fill my calendar back up.

The Guest List, Four

As soon as you get the list, review it. If she has fewer than a dozen people, call her and review the Top 40 list. She'll know you care. Remind her that having more people at her demonstration and getting more gifts takes the same amount of time as having just a few guests and getting just a few gifts (more guests, more gifts…see the correlation?).

Has she invited other people on her street? If you don't see any other people with her street address and she says she doesn't know any of the neighbors, suggest she go high tech–or ask if she minds if you do this simple step for her. Log on at www.msn.com or any other URL that might have the information I'm explaining here. Click on "white pages." Type in her name and address. If she's listed in the phone book, her name will pop up. Then, near her name, the words "neighbors of" (or something similar) will be listed. Click on those words. Now, you'll have a listing of all her neighbors! You can send a special note with the reminder. Here are some sentences you might use: "Lucky You! Your neighbor, _____ (her name), at _____ (her address), is hosting a ____ _____ (your company name) demonstration/party/show/workshop. Stop by and meet some new friends!

Isn't that simple? And, you just never know who her neighbors might be…your next host, recruit, leader? She'll love the extra service you provide. I don't explain this step initially because I want to keep the process simple. Only if I don't see neighbors listed do I suggest this.

Check to see if the list is in alphabetical order with more than 50 names. I remember the first time I got such a huge list and mailed out all the invites. I was disappointed when only three people showed up. Later, I found out the host simply went through the church/school/ neighborhood directory. She didn't call any of the people nor did she know any of them. There is nothing wrong with her using this as a resource as long as she has made some contact with them, and coded the list. (That's why the code system explained earlier works so well.)

Next, review the names to see if you know any of the people on the list. Some of these might be big fans of yours! Perhaps someone on the list is also someone in your Business Bank who has asked you to call this month. Go ahead and call her, get her date in your book, and give your host (the one who just mailed the list to you) credit for a booking. Wouldn't that be a fun surprise to tell her you already have a booking for her! Do you think she'll always want to be a host of yours? Of course!

If you see names of people you know well and know that they collect certain items from your product line, you'll want to bring some of them to surprise these people.

I call the host when I receive the list to let her know it's arrived and to thank her for her efforts. At that time, I might ask her to tell me about a couple of the guests on the list. Let me explain why this is so important. If I had this message typed out in Portuguese would you be able to read it? If you lived in Brazil or Portugal, you might. Would you go to a demonstration and speak a language that the guests didn't know? Of course not. If you plan a demonstration that is geared to say children under five and after you've finished, you discover that the host has young children but all the other people are empty nesters, it would have been as if you spoke a foreign language to them. If you get some general demographics of the people she's invited after you get the list, you'll be able to adapt your presentation to their situations. And the guests will love you for paying attention to their needs. Of course, sometimes you'll have a cross section of a variety of lifestyles. Remember: every situation is situational.

When I receive the Guest Lists, I create a file for that host. Her name is on the tab and she is placed in a vertical file that indicates I need to mail out the invitations/reminders. This way, I don't misplace a list.

Remember: names are worth millions! Are you feeling wealthy yet? Keep posted.

BONUS TIPS:
In appreciation to all of my great subscribers, I'm going to give you a bonus tip today–aside from how to build a business using the guest list. Your hosts will love this and so will you. When I share this idea at a Presentation$ for Profit live Learning Adventure, and I ask if anyone uses this tip, no one has. And this is dynamite...are you ready?

As soon as your new host puts a date on your calendar, before you even go over the Top 40 and other suggestions, ask her, "Do you have an answering machine or voice mail?" Most will reply in the affirmative. Suggest she revise her message right away so that it says something along these lines:

"Congratulations...you've reached _____ (host's name)! Have you heard the great news? I'm hosting a _____ (kind of party/ presentation) on _____ (day) at _____ (time). When you leave your message let me know who you'll be bringing with you! "

Is this simple or is this simple? And it is so effective. Think of all the people who will be calling your host's home from the time she books to the time of the presentation. One of my hosts received a call from the florist (her husband was sending her flowers and needed directions). The delivery person was ecstatic to hear about her demonstration; she had been looking for a consultant. Every day people will be calling her from doctor's offices to remind her about an appointment to people trying to sell her a new phone service. They might just need what you have to offer, and what other way are you going to reach them?

These are only "strangers". What about the friends she forgets to invite? It happens all the time. At the end of the show, she says, "I can't believe I forgot to invite Marge! We work out every morning together so I didn't put her name on my guest list, and I forgot to tell her!" If she had put this message on her voice mail, when Marge called, she would have known.

I promise you this tip is dynamite! To increase your business more and more continue to read, listen to, and use the ideas in the Lemon Aid books and tapes and be watching for an announcement of a NEW product with literally HUNDREDS more ideas of attracting–not attacking more hostesses. In the meantime, take advantage of the great sale before midnight tonight, the ideas in the current books and tapes are not posted on this list because I have too many new ones to share!

The Guest List, Five—The list has been received...now what?

Now you have this piece of paper–the guest list in your hands. What do you do with it? One question I'm frequently asked is: Who sends the mailing out...the host or the consultant. My answer: It depends. However if I could only choose one answer, I'd say the consultant. I'll list my reasons why and then give the times when I have the host take care of this.

Many people ask, "How do I get my host to give me a list?" The simple answer is positioning the request. Here are some words: "Sydney, one service I provide for all my hosts and customers is that I send out your printed invitations after you contact your friends. In order for me to do this, of course, I'll need a list from you with everyone's name, address, and phone number. Will you have an opportunity to compose, call, and code a list in the next three days? [Then we discuss when she can do this.] Since your date is on _____ (her date), I'll need to have the list back to me by _____." [The date of her presentation is what establishes the urgency for her to compose, call and code the list so that you can do your part.]

I can already read your mind: "How can I afford to send out 30 printed invitations when it's 37 cents a piece—that's over $10, plus the cost of the invitations!" (Or you might use postcards that cost less).

My first response is that you're looking at this as a cost rather than an investment in your business. Usually the people who complain about this the most are those who are willing to drop a hundred or more dollars to put a classified ad in a nickel newspaper in hopes that someone will read the ad and then call. Or, will not even think about spending more than that to have a booth at a fair or expo.

With a guest list, you have a targeted, hot market. The people on the list are friends and acquaintances of your host...not just names from a phone book. Direct marketers spend thousands and thousands of dollars to buy lists of names that are targeted, but cold. Then they spend thousands and thousands more to send out mailings that most people throw away! Do you realize what a valuable tool a guest list is and how you are investing practically nothing compared to your potential return? Can you tell I have strong convictions about this? And I haven't even begun to give you other ways to utilize the lists.

When I send out the printed invitations, I am in control. This is my business. I do this everyday. A host does not. She might forget to mail them, not have the money to buy the stamps, and so she cancels (of course she gives a different reason for doing so). Some consultants ask the host to send the postage or the cost of the postage to the consultant. This is TACKY! It reminds me of a grocery store I went to once (did you get the "once" part?). I had to give a deposit to use the cart and then I had to pay for the bags to put my groceries in. The service was non-existent and the prices weren't low enough to exchange for no service. A host might agree to this arrangement…once.

If you have the confidence in your business and your abilities, invest in your business. This is your advertising budget, and it's such effective advertising! If you have to use a credit card to buy the stamps and then pay the bill after you receive the profits, do so. I remember cutting back on my grocery budget to pay for the stamps (the post office didn't accept credit cards way back then). When all was said and done, my grocery budget and over all income increased because I was confident that with my great service, I'd earn many more times the amount of the postage. When you ask a host to assume your responsibility you're conveying, "I don't make enough money doing this, so you'll have to finance my business." Then, we talk about the "great opportunity" that we have? This is not congruent.

Now I'll come down off my Lemon Aid Stand to explain when I allow a host to hand out the invitations herself. When I call her to notify her that the list has arrived and she tells me most of the people work with her, many times she suggests handing out the printed invitations at work, school, or church. Or, if they are all in her neighborhood, sometimes she suggests hand delivering them. I do allow this *at her request*; I don't recommend it. Then I call her to be sure she's given them out. Nonetheless, I still have the list with the names, phones, and addresses.

The Guest List, Six—A *TWIST* on mailing the printed reminder

If you elect to do the mailing, do so 7-10 days in advance. This way, the people get them 5-7 days before the date. It allows for weekends, holidays, and mail delays. In most cases, this is the printed reminder, as you hope that she's already called or visited with her guests to invite them. Mail the host one also, so she knows that you have sent them out. On hers, send some more encouraging words.

I like to put something different on each mailer–different, but simple Here are a couple of things you can add:

1. I put a sticker that reads "Bring this card/brochure–you could be a wonderful winner." I use address labels to print this message, I don't hand write it. Using a number rubber stamp from an office supply store (this is like a date stamp, but has only numbers), I stamp a number on every piece, most with odd-ending numbers, and just a couple ending in an even number–say #8. I stamp the number right on the sticker telling them to bring the card with them. I like the numbers to be different so if they do compare with other invitees, they don't think I've "rigged" (even though I have, sort of!) At some point in the presentation, I ask to see who brought their reminder, and then I make a big deal about who has the "Wonderful Number." I simply ask who has a number that ends in an 8? and then I honor the people who have that "wonderful number" with a token remembrance–it could be your recruiting materials (isn't that the most valuable information you have?). The number has more meaning if there is some significance. For example, you could give eight reasons why everyone should join your company (quick ones, of course!). Or, you have eight items on sale today, etc.

2. Another idea is to stamp something seasonal (talk to our direct sales friends who sell these fun stamps) or use attractive stickers (call The Booster: 1-800-5JENNYB). On these I print a label that says, "Bring this card–match your stamp/sticker–you could be the winner." At the presentation, I have a sheet of paper with the winning stamp/sticker on it. As they come in, I invite them to see if they "match" the winner. This gets them up to your display right away looking at your products.

3. Or, print a label that says "Bring this Word Clue with You". Then write a word describing a particular product on each card. A couple of cards will have the winning word which is the name of a product. Let me illustrate. I just received my Mary Kay "The Look" from my consultant. She might put a word clue such as these on each card: "exhilarating" "euphoric" "fruity" "floral" "mangosteen" "tart" "banana" "clementine" "velocity" The first eight words are used to describe the fragrance "velocity." So, "velocity" is the winning word–it's the product. As I ask for people to name the word they have, it leads right into the demonstration and sample of this fragrance.

Note: On the last two illustrations, I used the word "card" in the generic sense. Your company might use brochures as their printed reminder/invitation.

Do you see why you, as the consultant, want to be in charge of mailing your written reminders? Putting the mailer together is very simple and the activity attached is very simple. Here are reasons why this tip is so effective: More people come to the presentation because they are curious, more people are recognized and rewarded, and the most important reason you'll want to do this is the current host and all potential hosts will see that getting you that guest list in a timely manner helps them have a more fun, successful presentation.

Lastly, the task of preparing and mailing these reminders is something you can do on downtime–while you're watching TV, laying out in the sun, waiting to pick up kids from school. Or, better yet, pay someone else to do this for you so you can use your time more wisely to book more shows and recruit and teach new people.

The Guest List, Seven—Here's where you'll see even more fun reasons for getting a Guest List

A couple of days before her presentation–usually two to three–I make my Random Request Calls. I randomly choose a few names off the list–usually one name for every eight to ten on the list. Then I call these people (now you know why I want the phone numbers, and this is another "persuasive point" for the host to get the list back to you).
Here's what I say:

> Jennifer! Hi! Christie calling from Northrup Party Plan [you put your name and company in here, of course]–I'm doing the party tomorrow night at Ruth Patterson's home. [Let her know this connection to the host right away so in her mind she's not thinking: "I've already been invited to a Northrup Party Plan."] Of all the many [you want her to feel special!] people Ruth invited, I've selected you to ask if you have any requests for me to bring a particular item that you want to see at the party tomorrow."

This is so incredibly effective! She feels so special! Maybe she's never seen your line before. This gives you a chance to find out about her and her lifestyle. Then you can suggest some things she might want. Or, she might say, "I've been dying to see that itsy-bitsy, teeny-weeny yellow polka dot picture frame…do you have that?" How many times have you just taken something out of your display and the next show someone asks to see it? This will eliminate that!

When you get to meet her in person, you both already know each other. And, when you demonstrate her "requested item", you can brag on her: "Thanks to Ruth, I brought along our famous itsy-bitsy, teeny-weeny yellow polka dot picture frame with me tonight."

Ruth is going to LOVE the recognition. People will ask how she was chosen to give a request. You can explain she was randomly selected and then add, "When you're a host, I let you help me design the demonstration—I bring what you want and when you return your guest list to me, I can also get some random requests from your guests."
Can you guess which guests will be requesting to be on you calendar? You're right! Those you met doing the random request phone calls.

118

The Guest List, Eight—The Lucky Winners

Here's a *TWIST* on the last idea–connecting with a few of the guests before you meet them in person at the presentation. In order to do this fun activity, you need to have the completed guest list from your host–meaning the names, phones, and addresses of those she has invited.

A few days before her date, I choose a couple Lucky Winners. For every eight to ten people on the list, I call one person. If I see thirty names, I tell myself the lucky numbers today are 16, 20, and 4 (you choose your own numbers). Then I count down the list: 1, 2, 3, 4–she's a lucky winner, and so on. The more people on the list, the more people who will be the Lucky Winners.

Here's what I say when I dial: "Lorraine! Christie calling from Northrup Party Plan...I'm doing the show at Diane's this Friday evening! Guess What? Of all the people Diane invited, you have been chosen as one of our Lucky Winners! As soon as you walk in the door, run up to me and say 'I'm a Lucky Winner–I'll have something special for you!'"

You'll have some dialog here with her, of course. There are also a lot of "what ifs?" One of the biggest is when she says, "Darn, I have bowling that night and I can't come." Then I say, "No problem, when you schedule your own show, I'll bring the 'something special' right to your home! And you can invite all the people you bowl with." Does she jump at this chance to be a host? Not always, but a lot of people will accept your offer. If you hadn't have done this activity, you wouldn't have met Lorraine at all.

When the "Lucky Winners" do arrive, award them with something very valuable–but not expensive. These people already have a connection with you. They are flattered and excited that they were chosen as the Lucky Winner. Guess who will be among the first to be your next host? The Lucky Winners! It works! It also shows the future hosts the importance of getting the list to you.

The Guest List, Nine

As a member of nearly every hotel "frequent stayer" club, I love the one special perk I get when I check in: My room key card folder is in a special, plastic see-through, wall holder reserved just for the frequent stayers. The reservation is already processed. I know they've been expecting me, and I feel like a VIP.

How can we give our party guests the same welcome feeling that they are very important persons when they arrive? First, you have to get a completed guest list back from the hostess. If you print out mailing labels with each person's name and address, print out two sets. Of course, one will go on the printed mailer.

Are you ready for the Lemon Aid *TWIST*? The second set of labels will be used to put on each person's order form. You'll keep these order forms in the valuable file folder where you store the guest list. When you go to the demonstration, you'll take these personalized order forms with you. As you meet and greet each guest, you will present her with this personalized gift–the order form that is waiting for her, complete with her address. What does this convey–rather than out right say? It conveys, "I've been expecting you." Don't we all like to think people have been awaiting our presence? Sure we do. We all like to feel wanted and appreciated.

Another benefit is she doesn't have to write out all this information–you've done the work for her. All she has to do is order! And, she'll probably feel more like ordering when you've made the task simple for her!

I know you have some questions about this terrific *TWIST*. Let me answer them before you can ask.

What happens if the people don't come?
This technique is great because after the show, when you're sitting down with your host to review the sales, simply hand her the order forms and explain these are the people she invited who did not attend. You already have the order forms started, all she has to do is call the people to get their orders. She might even have some pre-party orders from them and you only have to transfer them.

What if they don't come or order?
Won't I be wasting a lot of order forms? You won't waste anything because there is no law dictating how many labels you can stick on top of one another.

If I only put one label on the order form, but my order form has three copies, what do I do?
The bottom copy is normally given to the guest that evening. She probably doesn't care that her name isn't on it. The middle copy normally is left with the host for packing the order. Bring an extra set of labels (so you'll initially print out three sets) to put on the hostesses' copy. Of course, every company and order form is different, you should be able to adapt easily with these suggestions.

What if someone comes who was not listed on the guest list?
Personally write in her information for her. When you "ink it, not just think it," you'll remember her name.

An added benefit is you'll actually be able to read the name on the order forms! Sometimes people write quickly and sloppily.

The best benefit is your guests will feel special. And when they feel special, they will want a repeat performance from you–they'll schedule a workshop and won't question you when you ask for a guest list to be returned because they will have felt the benefits and will want their guests to feel the same.

Guest List, Ten

Have you ever prepared a lovely dinner for your family and they ate it all–no leftovers! I love when that happens because clean up is so easy! However, I normally plan meals so I have leftovers (which are really plan-overs) and thus, another meal. This process not only saves time in the future, but also allows me not to have to think of "what's for dinner" in an upcoming day or two.

What does this have to do with using a guest list to build your business? Keep reading. Have you ever gone to a home demonstration and everyone who the host invited came and ordered? This is a rarity in our industry. Normally a third of the people who the host invites will attend, and then another third will usually place an order. From these two groups, you can usually get about three new presentations scheduled. What about the other third of the people who didn't attend or order–the so-called "leftovers"? That's what this post is all about.

You wouldn't leave good food sitting on the table after dinner, nor would you flush good food down the garbage disposal. However, when you do nothing with the names that are on the guest list whose lives you have not touched, you are throwing names, business, and potential profits away. And more importantly, the people are not being serviced, receiving gifts, or becoming your new friend.

After a presentation is over, I encourage the host to call those who have not attended or ordered to see if they want something (remember the previous post about having the order forms ready for these types). Sometimes the host will even beg them to book a demonstration if she is working for a goal and needs it. Do all hosts call back all people? Of course not! But you can–if you have the guest list with the phone numbers.

What do you say? It's very simple. "Cathy! Christie calling from Northrup Parties. I missed meeting you at Merrilee's last night." She'll proceed to tell you why she didn't come. She might even say, "I hate home parties." Or, I have so many Northrup Products, I just don't need any more."

Let her do this so you can assess her temperature about your company and product. If this is the case (which it will be often–they don't like/want/need your product) just listen. Do not try to "overcome her objection." She might tell you she had other commitments, she was too tired, etc. etc. etc. Whatever she says, simply reply: "Since you were unable to join us,

I'm calling to invite you to be a hostess with me." Then...listen. If she says a flat out NO!, simply tell her you hope to meet her in the future.

On the other hand, she might say YES! More often than not, her schedule prevented her attendance. Because I personally contacted her, I discovered a better time or season for me to connect in the future, and then I followed through appropriately. In other words, these "names on a paper" now became real people–and future profits to all involved. Believe it or not, I scheduled many a demonstration by calling these "leftovers" back. Sometimes, they were better than the original meal (demonstration). Names truly are worth millions… millions of new bookings, referrals, sales, and mostly millions of new friends!

Guest List, Eleven—Keep in a safe place

During the past weeks, I have shared many ways that a host list can benefit you, your hosts, and her guests. Remember, all are working on the same team. One does not benefit while the other profits. It's a three-way win: the guests have special attention, you sell and book more, and your host has a better turn out. And there is still one other way all three parties involved benefit; this shows up months (hopefully) and maybe even years later.

I hope your goal is to have hosts for life. This means, whenever a host schedules with you and you do your presentation, your hosts are so loyal to you that they would never ever think of having another consultant from your company except you–unless, of course, they join your team! One way to insure this is to give extra service and that's where a guest list comes in.

While I've been putting these posts out, I've had many great questions from the Lemon Aid Learners. One is the fear that the host will not want to take the time to get her friends' addresses and phone numbers together. However, when she sees that you are using some of the tips I've already shared (preparing labels for their order forms, mailing the printed reminders, doing random request calls, etc.), she'll see the value to her and to her guests, and she won't question your suggestion. Also, when you have the information once, you'll not have to get the same information again–even though she'll have many, many more parties with you.

You do this by holding on to each host's guest list and keeping it in a safe place. My suggestion is a simple file folder; one for each host. In this folder, I put everything pertaining to that host; including her guest list. In about six months, I'll call my host to see if she is ready to have another demonstration with me. When she excitedly agrees, I can speed things up. I already have her guest list in front of me; she can start at step two rather than step one. I let her know I have her guest list already and then say, "All we need to do is update and add to the list you already have." I cannot tell you how surprised my hosts were when they knew I kept their information. Of course I did. Remember, names are worth

MILLIONS. Now you have millions of compliments from happy hosts, and you'll have MILLIONS more new bookings because they know when they are your host, you make having a presentation easy for them. They love this extra service.

Additionally, when you review her guest list, you are also updating your customer database. For example, when you read off the names, she will let you know who has moved and will give you the new address if she has it. Plus, you can assure her that even if her friends have moved out of the area, you can still send a catalog to them (at your expense; after all you'll benefit greatly) in their new town. Who knows, maybe that person will join your team because she might not have a consultant from your company in her new city.

You can also find out other info about your customers because as you review the list, your current host will tell you about new babies, weddings, even deaths and divorces. This personal touch really builds your business. Companies, including mine, spend hours and hours updating customer data. Your host can be your assistant in helping you manage and build yours–all while she's having fun and earning great gifts from you!

What would you do...and how much would you pay...to have a list of your *future* hostesses? This, in essence is what you have in your hands when you work with a host to create a guest list. You not only have a sheet a paper with the names/addresses/phone numbers of people she's invited, but you also have a list of your future hostesses!

I want to end with two ideas:

1. If you've attended my Lemon Aid Learning Adventure, Presentation$ 4 Profit, you'll know I believe we should focus on the people in attendance not merely our product. So, here's another way to do so. Make a photocopy of the guest list. Cut it up so you have each name/address individually. Put them in an envelope and take these to the party with you.

   Rather than doing "drawings" where the guests have to fill anything out (we know they really don't enjoy extra paper work), simply use these slips of paper for any drawing or recognition. Note: rather than leave them in the paper envelope, unless you sell paper envelopes, put the slips in one of your products.

   Or, put each slip inside/on top/next to/or taped to a product on your display table. As they come in, direct them to the table to find what product you paired them with–great way to get them looking at your display right away. When you're ready for the demonstration, have each guest share what they would use the product for. You'll learn quickly who would be a great new consultant. Be ready to guide each person so they will not be embarrassed.

2. A personal experience: A hostess had a "Sour Situation" and had no choice but to cancel her show with me. I can't remember exactly why, but it was something devastating like an illness or death of a relative. She called me panicking; she did not have time or the energy to call all the people she knew would show up at her home. She didn't want everyone to drive to her home just to find a note hanging on the door.

When she called, I assured her everything would be taken care of. I quickly pulled out her guest list and called everyone. While I had them on the phone, I was able to get orders for things they had planned on buying as well as scheduled more demonstrations. After all, when the guests saw that I was so willing to help their friend, they knew I would service them well also.

In the end, in spite of her personal "Sour Situation" I was able to do the *TWIST* and she still ended up having successful, profitable gifts. She became a hostess for life because we had a back up plan—we had worked together and created a valuable guest list; which ended up paying dividends for everyone involved: host, guest, consultant. This is truly a GRAND SLAM, WIN/WIN/WIN way to build people as you build your business.

Do They Remember You?

Common knowledge tells us that knowing our guests' names is effective in booking more classes and bonding business relationships. In addition to knowing your guests' names, do they know your name? If I came to your office and dialed the phone numbers of everyone who had ever ordered from you, and asked the customer/hostess, "Can you tell me who your _____ (company) Consultant is?" My guess is that at least half of the people do not remember *your name*. And, what if they wanted to get in touch with you to order product or book a show? How are they going to remember who you are?

The biggest challenge of marketing is getting your customers' attention and then keeping it. Your customers will remember you because of one of three things:

You have the distinction of being the first. Of course, this means the first ever consultant in the company, *or* this could mean the first consultant in your company who they've met.

You are the best. Perhaps you are the number one selling consultant or leader in your company, or even on your street! Tell the world you're the best!

If you don't fit in either of the above categories, you can definitely fit in the third: **Be different!**

Last week, my husband and I were on a business and family trip. We took our son to find an apartment out of state where he'll be attending college. During this trip, I was able to visit my parents who live about an hour from my son's new apartment. In talking with my dad, he reminisced about his experience of leaving the safety of his hometown and venturing to the "big city" to seek employment soon after high school graduation.

My dad was interested in business, and although at the time did not have a college degree, he was able to get a very good office job at the railroad because he knew shorthand. Some of you reading this might not know what shorthand means. It's a method for taking dictation word for word in a very fast manner. With today's technology, some feel the need for shorthand is non-existent. However, my dad continues to use this skill and throughout his corporate career was well-known and respected because of this talent. His position at the railroad over 50 years ago has opened many doors for him throughout his successful business career. All because he had a skill very few men knew. In fact, my sisters and I learned shorthand mostly so we could read the notes and grocery lists he'd write!

My father, who some called "Shorthand Stan," has a unique skill and capitalized on it. You have something unique about you. Do you know what it is? Perhaps you have a unique skill as well. Maybe your name sets you apart from others. Do you have an interest or even an e-mail address that connects and identifies you with your business, which will create a difference so people remember you?

You all know me as The Lemon Aid Lady. Some of you might not even know my real name. That's okay. Because when you experience Sour Situations in your direct sales business, I want you to remember to contact The Lemon Aid Lady so you can *TWIST* the Sour Situation into Sweet Successes and Juicy Profits!

My father's shorthand and my being known as The Lemon Aid Lady are examples of personal icons. What is your personal icon? What makes you different from other consultants–in and out of your company? Sure, you might be known as the "Candle Lady" or the "Basket Lady" etc., but so are thousands of other people. What can you "rename" yourself–as I did with The Lemon Aid Lady–or how can you position yourself with a slogan, etc. so that *your hostesses and customers remember you whenever they think of your company or category*?

Who Are You?
How do you introduce yourselves to your guests as you begin your presentation? For years, I stood up and said my name, how long I'd been with the company…yada, yada, yada. The same old stuff that everyone says! Then I did the *TWIST* and asked my hostesses to introduce me.

At hostess planning time, I asked her if she minded reading my introduction. Although no one ever said "no" don't assume she will. And definitely don't put her on the spot by asking her to read your introduction when you get to the party. Next, I asked her why she decided to book a party with me.

Now, I put a script together that reads something like this:

"Welcome to my _____ Party everyone! The best part of our demonstration is our consultant, _____ (your name). I met her at _____ (hostess she booked from). I decided to have my own party because _____ (this could be a product she wants to qualify for, she liked how you did the last demonstration, she wants to show off her new house/baby, etc.).
_____ (your name) has been with _____ (company name) for _____ (months and/or years). She has been recognized as (trips you've won, awards received, etc.) OR…. She loves working with _____ (company name) because _____ _____ (why you love what you do). Let's all welcome, _____ [clap, clap, clap], our _____ consultant/demonstrator/representative.

Believe it or not, your hostess' friends will believe what she says more than they believe what you tell them. Let them tell their friends about the gifts they want to earn and "brag" on you.

If you're brand new, and haven't received recognition or earned trips, etc., and if you want to know how to recognize a previous hostess, AND understand how having a hostess introduce you will add more recruits to your team, read pages 53-60 in *Presentations for Profit$*.

Thank U, Two—Testimonials for more bookings!

The biggest difference between retail and direct sales marketing is in direct sales, we advertise via word of mouth–the most effective form of advertising in any industry. When we think of "word of mouth" we most often think of our friends telling their friends who tell their friends about our business. That works; however, here's a *TWIST* on whose mouths spread the word.

The first person your hostess should invite to her class is the person she booked from. Because the "Previous Hostess" probably received credit in gifts for the booking, she'll most likely be anxious to attend. As a consultant, you want her to attend for another reason: to share a Totally Terrific Testimonial!

After you've thanked your hostess in front of her friends (I hope you all do this), you want to take the thanks one step further and Thank U, Two! Here's what to say:

"Before we begin, there's another person here tonight that I want to thank. In fact, if it weren't for her, none of us would be here. Please welcome Claire...the person Jessica [tonight's hostess] scheduled her class from. Claire, come on down !

[Claire is surprised and happy that she's recognized and stands next to me and I continue]

Claire, thanks to you, we're all here at Jessica's to learn more about _____ (class/workshop/party topic)! Do you mind if I ask you a couple of questions? [I've never had anyone say "no."]

Claire, did you enjoy being a hostess? Did your friends enjoy the ideas they learned? Were you rewarded with any gifts?"

As I'm "interviewing" Claire, she's giving her Totally Terrific Testimonial about her experience as a hostess. In essence, she's booking more parties for me because she's relating that it was fun, enjoyable, and rewarding. So, instead of your having to explain how your hostess gift program works, the guests are hearing from someone who has benefited from being a hostess. What another guest says has more impact and believability than what you tell.

The last question I always ask the Previous Hostess, as I present her with a remembrance of her party, is "Are you looking forward to being a hostess again?"

Thank U, Two not only gives additional recognition to your previous hostess, but encourages more previous hostesses to attend the bookings from their class, motivates more guests to book with you, and secures more re-bookings...all in a fun way with a *TWIST*!

Time is Money. . . and More Bookings!

Have you ever heard the reply, "I don't have time" when you've invited someone to be a hostess? I believe these words rank in the top five reasons for people to "say no to parties." So, let's do the Lemon Aid *TWIST*.

Next time you hear those words, mentally add two more words to the end of the sentence– "to waste." I believe that most people are saying, "I don't have time *to waste*." They are more concerned about wasting time rather than making time to host a presentation. We all make time to do the things we really want to do–and see the value in doing. As consultants, rather than "overcoming the objection," we can actually add value to hostess' and guests' time by:

Beginning on Time: If your hostess asks you to "wait for a few more people," offer to give those who are already present some fun, Value Added Tips–something you hadn't planned to share. The people who are on time should not be penalized for people who are "on their way" (and sometimes never arrive). Likewise, never make someone feel bad for coming late; be happy they came! More people will book because you are respecting their time by adding value.

Dynamic Demonstrations in Time: How long is your demonstration? Are you keeping the guests' attention? If people begin mentally drifting, they'll feel their time is being wasted. These are they who say, I don't have time (to waste). Can you teach what you need to in a shorter amount of time?

End on Time: Face it, the biggest chunk of time is usually the ordering session. People are visiting, eating, etc. So, do what the stores do, announce, "Ladies, I'll be here until 8:30 [or whatever time you decide; this is just a suggestion] to help you with your orders. I promised Beth we'd wrap up by then so she can get her babies to bed." Okay, the stores say, "We're closing, bring your purchases to the check out." This is essentially what you're saying...with a Lemon Aid *TWIST*!

As we welcome an entire year of time into our lives in just a couple of weeks, do all you can do to add value to guests' and hostess' time; you won't be hearing "I don't have time" much longer.

Window Shoppers to Committed Customers

Do you give out hundreds–maybe thousands–of catalogs every year and wonder why you don't get any or more orders from them? Let me give you a few hints that will *TWIST* the window shoppers (just looking at a catalog) into orders and committed customers:

1. When you send a catalog, INCLUDE AN ORDER FORM (even if it's just a photocopy of the order form). This sends the message that you expect an order, not just a window shopper. If an order form is part of your catalog, attach a sticky note (the skinny strip kind are good) so it hangs out the side of the catalog, write "order here" on it.

2. Write the person's name, phone, and address on the order form (you have this information for those that you're mailing). When her name is on the order form, she feels ownership right away and is more likely to take action.

3. If the tax is based on your tax rate, include a tax chart (very inexpensive to reproduce) or fill in the tax rate. If the tax is based on where she lives, write "your tax rate" next to the tax box.

4. Highlight or circle shipping/handling info so she can see it easily.

5. Indicate who/company name the check is to be written to. Highlight which, if any, credit cards you accept.

6. Put a handwritten note telling her when to expect delivery/pickup. "You will be enjoying these producs approximately two weeks after I've received your order."

7. Give customers more than one way to get the order to you: a. Calling you on the phone (a 24/7 dedicated business line is best; advertise she can order at any time by leaving a message) b. Faxing the order (again a dedicated 24/7 line) c. Your website d. Mailing the order to you (be sure to include your mailing address).

8. If the order was received without your talking with the customer, contact her to confirm the order, thank her, and reiterate the delivery. And, of course to offer her the privilege of being a hostess and using this order as the first order or a free order

These are simple ways to convey "place an order" rather than just "look at the catalog." The easier you make placing an order, the more orders customers will place. If, after the customer has had the catalog for more than a week, you haven't received an order, call her. Think of the times you've received a catalog. Your intentions are to order, but that phone is oh...so HEAVY and you're oh...so BUSY. See, our customers are just like us...lots of good intentions, then it's too late. This idea will build sales away from your demonstrations.

If you want ways to add profits to your presentations, take a look at my book *Presentations for Profit$:* A dozen ways to increase bookings at Home Party demonstrations.

What Hostesses & Guests Really Want
One of the most rewarding parts of being a home party consultant is playing Santa all year round! Do you ever feel like giving the gifts to a deserving hostess is almost more fun than getting gifts yourself?

Gift promotions are a key part of a home party business. As I consultant I loved giving thousands and thousands of dollars of product away. And, as a hostess, I love being the recipient of hostess gifts. I believe most consultants and hostesses share my feelings. So, why don't more and more people book classes and shows from you if the gift program is so wonderful? Because, believe this next statement or not, gifts are not the only reason why people are persuaded to be a hostess. Yet, they're usually the main "crutch" we use for booking.

Since December, I've given you a half a dozen of very specific, easy ideas that most of you have never heard of or used before to attract–not attack–more hostess at our demonstrations. Never in any of the messages did I suggest badgering, begging or bribing as ways to attract more hostesses. This is not to imply that gifts are a mode of badgering, begging or bribing. However, all the ancillary things consultants themselves add can be; many times these confuse rather than compensate a hostess…

So, what do hostess and guests really want from you as a consultant? I believe **they want you to pay**…not for gifts or gadgets–but to pay…**attention to them and their specific needs and requests**.

They want the gift of your presence…not just your presents. This gift means you give them what they cannot purchase or qualify for. They want a consultant who forgets her own needs and goals when she's at a party and discovers and then focuses on the wants and wishes of her audience. A consultant with presence is professional in her personal, paper, and product "packaging." She's punctual by arriving–and leaving–on time. She's knowledgeable about her products and opportunities, but doesn't tell everything she knows at one show. She entertains and educates her guests in a fun, non-threatening, non-aggressive manner. A consultant with presence follows through on promises from answering questions, to returning defective product, to calling and keeping in touch. **Guests and hostesses feel blessed for having had the experience of her presentation– and presence–and are thirsty for more!**

If you are using only your Hostess Gift program to book parties, you might be encountering Booking Barriers. I know all about those! It took doing the Lemon Aid *TWIST* to break through my personal Booking Barrier…more about that on page 103 of *Presentations for Profit$: Dozens of ways to increase bookings at Home Party demonstrations* (for details on the book, visit www.lemonaidlady.com.

Give Your Goal Away

Last week I gave a *TWIST* on what most hostesses and guests really want. Today I'll give you another *TWIST* on hostess gifts.

Are you setting a weekly and monthly sales goal? If not, you won't achieve the goal… you'll just end up someplace—who knows where. If you have set those goals, are you telling everyone what that goal is? I hope not. People really don't care. Sure they like to hear of your successes; everyone loves to work with a successful consultant. But if you make your sales goal or not, is not of importance to them.

So, do the Lemon Aid *TWIST*. Rather than announcing your sales goal, make a big deal about your gift goal–how much you're *giving away*! Here's how. Decide on your sales goal, then determine how many demonstrations, using your personal show average, you'll need to achieve it. Let's say your goal works out to holding ten shows a month. If you give away an average of $200.00 of product at your average party, your Gift Goal is to give

away $2,000.00 this month. (Note: If your goal is to hold just one class a week, you might want to establish a quarterly goal.) Big numbers are impressive to people. Better to say, "I'm giving away $2,000 this quarter" than "I'm giving away $650.00 this month."
At your parties, announce: "This month my goal is to give away $2,000 worth of _____. So far, I've given away $650! How much of the remaining $1,350 would you like?"

This suggestion accomplishes a couple of things. First and most importantly, you're focusing on their benefit—not yours!

Think about this: Have you ever received a Sweepstakes offer in the mail from the magazine companies (i.e. Publisher's Clearinghouse). How do they get your attention to enter the sweepstakes? Do they say, "Our goal is to sell 2.5 million magazine subscriptions?" No, they say, "You may have already won 50 Million Dollars!" Now, that gets your attention… you see immediately what you might win—even though the chances are slim.

Next, you convey a definite dollar amount of gifts. Let's say as the month goes on, you've already given away $2,000 of free product. Do you close your business? No, you do the *TWIST*: "I've already exceeded my give away goal for the month by awarding my hostesses with over $2,000 of free _____. However, I have permission from my company to increase by gift goal by another $500.00—how much of this will you want when you book and hold your class this month?"

You can also use these words when phoning: "Gloria, Great News! _____ (company) has authorized me to give away $2,000 of free _____ this month! How much of that do you want to receive as a hostess?"

Take your eye off of your goal, focus on what you can give, rather than get, and you'll get a whole lot more. For other ideas of this subject, read pages 101 in *Presentations for Profit$*. It's the book you'll want to read if you want more bookings.

Don't Give This to Your Hostess

Last week I gave you a *TWIST* on giving your goal away. Today I'll share what hostesses don't want. When you realize this, you'll book more parties. I'll begin with a couple of illustrations.

My good friend called the other day, and she was quite upset. She just moved to a newly built home and had her security system activated. The salesman was eager to make the sale (as we all are) and filled out the paperwork on her brand new, gorgeous, cherry wood dining table. After all the paperwork was completed and the transaction finalized the salesman left. He also left an imprint of the contract engraved on her new table!

Your hostess does not want any imprints of sales receipts or order forms or drawing slips left on any of her furniture. Always have some sort of a pad to write on. And, don't let this pad be one of her books–they don't need an imprint either. Bring your own portable desk (i.e. a clipboard) or use your catalogs to write on.

As a new recruit was accompanying me to a demonstration, I was impressed that she had dressed so professionally. She wore a nice suit and high heels. The next day I got a call from my hostess. My new consultant's heels left "dimples" on the hostess' new wood flooring. I was mortified! Her insurance company was covering the floor replacement; I offered to pay the deductible. She wouldn't allow that, but she also never had another party with me. I actually didn't ask her why; I was too embarrassed.

When guests come to my home, I ask them to take off their shoes; it's something we've always done. So, I got in the habit of asking my hostess if she had the same policy in her house–many people do. I began bringing nice slippers so I didn't look too casual. My hostesses appreciated this. Guests followed my example, and in a few cases, I even did an impromptu "Sock it to me" Featured Attraction!

When setting up displays, always ask permission to place items anywhere besides the table she's provided. I loved setting items around the room, not just on the display table. If I put something on a coffee table, I ask permission. Many times I didn't use a table, but rather a kitchen bar or fireplace hearth. If the products are being placed on her table, be sure to cover it with a tablecloth. Have one handy in with your products. A suggestion is to go to a fabric store and buy 2-3 yards of washable fabric in different colors for a table covering. I had different fabrics for different holidays or featured attractions.

Remember: As party plan professionals, we are invited guests at people's homes. Always respect her home as if it were your own. My motto: Always give the hostess and guests more than what they expect; and, don't give them what they don't want (scratched furniture, dirty carpet, etc.).

Chapter Nineteen: Recruiting – Sharing Your Business Success

What Comes First–Booking, Selling, or Sharing?

It's a question often asked: Which came first, the chicken or the egg? With spring approaching and chickens, eggs, and other Easter decorations in sight, here's how this question can be the answer to your business growth.

Let me tell you how I recruited hundreds of people. When I met someone at a demonstration or at any other of the many, many places where I found customers or hostesses,* when they expressed or gained a love and passion for my product, I invited them to look at the business plan. Now, which is the "chicken" in this scenario, and which is the "egg?"

Most people believe a customer wouldn't have an interest in having a business if they didn't love the product. Or, some might think if a guest doesn't want to be a hostess, s/he wouldn't want to know about the income plan. I know I had this mentality for years. I looked at the business as the chicken–an end result, when it is really the egg—a golden, reproductive egg at that!

When Dave Longaberger began selling his baskets via the home party plan, he already had a product. His baskets were the "chicken," or the end result. (I highly recommend his book, *Longaberger: An American Success Story*, to everyone–especially everyone involved in a Party Plan business.) On the other hand, when Mary Kay Ash began her company, she had the "egg," which was a business plan. She just needed a product to market. (And, I'll recommend her book, *Mary Kay on People Management*.) Both individuals began their thriving companies for two different reasons, just as people join our businesses for a myriad of reasons.

For years, I lead people into the business with the "chicken" (the product) and then presented them with the "egg" (the business plan). Then I did the *TWIST*. Believe it or not, I discovered some people actually cared more about building a business and making a substantial income than if they loved the product. These people began with the egg and hatched chickens–which produced more eggs and more chickens and…

Don't misunderstand me. I don't believe I ever recruited someone who wasn't impressed with the product and used it. But, I learned that passion for the plan could be stronger than passion for the product! I discovered those who hatched their egg right away (the ones convinced that the business was a viable income opportunity) had more longevity and productivity than those who had a chicken and hoped it would lay eggs (those who loved the product and crossed their fingers that others who also loved the products would just maybe look at the business aspect).

Recently in a consulting session, one of my Lemon Aid Learners, who is a consultant for a company launching a new concept, shared that she was frustrated because she had to first get people hooked on the concept (the chicken) before she could talk about the business (the egg). I suggested she do the *TWIST* and teach people about the opportunity and then share information about the product. She hadn't thought of this before; there are plenty of people in the same basket! Many direct sellers think like the "real" world where we go up the ladder: guest, hostess, and consultant. We're in a progressive industry! We don't have ladders…we have eggs!

One of listings I always suggest be on your Top 40 List** as well as your Getting to Know You slip*** is "Someone looking for a career/job change." A top leader in one of the largest party plan companies politely questioned this. She indicated that most of her recruits came into the business because they liked the product and wanted it at a discount. I didn't disagree at all. I was simply suggesting the *TWIST.* Begin looking for individuals who are shopping for an economic plan (the egg), not only a popular product (the chicken).

Whichever way you choose to hatch new business (I suggest both), just don't be CHICKEN about sharing, or you won't hatch any EGGS!

For a fun, "eggfective" way to talk about your business opportunity, read pages 73-75 and 95-96 in Presentations for Profit$: Dozens of ways to increase bookings at Home Party demonstrations." If you don't have your copy, visit www.lemonaidlady.com.

*Refer to the Lemon Aid Lead Alphabet: Where to Find Customers when you run out of Family and Friends
**Refer to Presentations for Profit$, pages 3-6
***Refer to Presentations for Profit$, pages 80-84

The Really Smart Mom
Once upon a time there was a Really Smart Mom. She lived in a nice little house and had three darling children. She worked very hard all day keeping her home nice and raising her children. Money was tight for this family, but the Really Smart Mom didn't want to leave her children to go out and get a job. So she happily–and sometimes wearily–kept doing what she was doing.

Really Smart Mom had three neighbors: Mrs. Boring, Dee Mize, and Whiney Butz. These three neighbors were also moms. Every morning they got together, had their doughnuts and coffee, and watched *Regis and Kelly* before spending the rest of the day viewing soap operas. Every morning they complained about how life was so hard, money was scarce, and children so difficult. Really Smart Mom didn't have time to join them. She was busy strengthening her family and caring for her home.

One day, Really Smart Mom got a gift in the mail: an invitation to a home party from her friend in the next town! She was excited to join her friends, see the newest products, and hear creative ideas. The invitation said she could "bring a friend and receive a gift." So, she called her neighbors:

Mrs. Boring said, "Not I. I'm not going to drive that far"

Dee Mize said, "Not I. I'd rather shop at K'ame-A-Part."

Whiney Butz said, "Not I. I have no money to buy anything."

So Really Smart Mom went by herself.

At the Home Party, Really Smart Mom had a really great time! The Kind Consultant made her feel important and was very informed about the products and shared great tips. And, without any pressure, but pure interest, Kind Consultant invited Really Smart Mom to be a hostess. Really Smart Mom–because she was really smart–happily agreed!

The next day, Really Smart Mom told the neighbors the good news. She invited them to come to her party–right there in the neighborhood:

Mrs. Boring said, "Not I. I'll probably be busy watching TV reruns!"

Dee Mize said, "Not I. Those parties are so boring!"

Whiney Butz said, "Not I. I have no money to buy anything."

So Really Smart Mom invited other friends, families and neighbors. The Kind Consultant did such a fabulous presentation. Everyone enjoyed the party so much, many wanted to attend again–especially when Kind Consultant gave them previews of coming attractions! In fact, four people scheduled their own demonstrations!

Kind Consultant was not only kind, but also very generous. Rather than hoarding new hostesses and business, she knew her business would grow more when she shared it. So, Kind Consultant invited Really Smart Mom to join her company. Really Smart Mom was excited to learn she had qualified for more than $200 worth of free merchandise! And when Kind Consultant revealed what her profit was from the party, Really Smart Mom made a really smart decision and said, "I will, I will."

The next morning Really Smart Mom told her neighbors the really great news. Because she was really smart, she invited them all to be hostesses so they could have fun and profit from free products:

135

Mrs. Boring said, "Not I. I don't 'do' parties."

Dee Mize said, "Not I. I don't want to pressure my friends."

Whiney Butz said, "Not I. My house is too small and I have no money to buy anything."

Really Smart Mom was really smart because she didn't listen to their responses. She went about caring for her home and children and now building her new business.

Really Smart Mom made money right away. This pleased Really Smart Dad. And the Really Smart kids were happy because Really Smart Mom was happy; they enjoyed the time they had alone with their Really Smart Dad when Really Smart Mom was working on her business.

Because of the example of her leader, Kind Consultant, Really Smart Mom also shared her business with other people. In fact, she saw that so many other people were benefiting from the business. She invited her neighbors to join her.

Mrs. Boring said, "Not I. This sounds like one of those illegal schemes—you're making too much money for this to be real."

Dee Mize said, "Not I. I'm not a pushy sales person."

Whiney Butz said, "Not I. I don't have any money to start a new business—and my husband wouldn't let me.

The Really Smart Mom was really smart and didn't listen to her friends. She continued to care for her home and children and to build her business.

One day, Really Smart Mom had a really big celebration. She had earned a promotion in her company! As the months and years went by, she saved enough money to buy a larger home in a new neighborhood (it even had a swimming pool!). Her children were so excited! They'd each have their own rooms. Her husband was delighted. He would have a huge garage. And Really Smart Mom was pleased and so thankful that her business gave her such an awesome opportunity to be a Really Smart Mom and a Really Successful Consultant.

On moving day, when the big moving van was packing and loading the Really Smart Family's possessions, Really Smart Mom's neighbors came over.

"We can't wait to come and visit you in your Really Wonderful new home! When will you invite us over? We'll bring our kids so we can all go swimming in your pool."

Really Smart Mom–who by now was also really wise–told them: "You weren't interested in what I was doing when I started my business. You criticized me for my choices and were never supportive. You wasted so much time complaining and never wanted to see anything positive in life. Now, you can do what you've always wanted–stay right where you are."

The Really Smart Mom was right. She didn't listen to people when they weren't supportive. She focused on strengthening her family first and growing her business. And now, she could choose to surround herself with her Really Smart Family and Totally Terrific Sales Team and enjoy many Sweet Successes and Juicy Profits!

Chapter Twenty: Run Your Business AS a Business

Business Like a Root Canal

For nearly two years, I had not chewed on the left side of my mouth. Every time something hot touched my bottom left molar, I felt terrible pain. Finally, I went to the dentist (one of my least favorite places). He advised that I needed a root canal...in case you don't know, a tooth needing a root canal is sensitive to heat. I finally made an appointment with an endodontist (root canal doctor). However, as the time drew nearer, I found an excuse why I just couldn't go in. So, I cancelled the appointment. The real reason was FEAR!

Because of my busy travel schedule, I finally made another appointment ten months later. I tried to find an excuse for canceling that appointment, but I was AFRAID the doctor would discover my FEAR was keeping me from her chair. Finally, the week before Thanksgiving, I mustered enough courage to put myself in the dentist chair. I "invited" my son to drive me so I'd have some company (real meaning: I was hoping he'd rescue me from the dentist chair!). That appointment was an hour and a half long. The doctor did some testing to be sure I needed the procedure done, and then described what she needed to do. She was very kind and gentle, but I was very defensive. There must be a catch if she's so nice, don't you agree? I was offered nitrous oxide to help me relax during the process, but declined (I'm so brave!). The shot of numbing medicine worked very well. I really didn't feel anything. The only discomfort was what I heard (the drilling), not felt. I actually survived the first appointment.

Now I had another eight weeks until my schedule would mesh with the doctor's to complete the procedure. That came two weeks ago. This time, my good husband volunteered to drive me. I told him that I had the confidence to be on my own, but I always enjoy his company. I even took a cassette recorder with headphones and some tapes to listen to so I wouldn't hear the drilling and grinding of the dentist's tools. The hardest part of this appointment was sitting still for two hours and keeping my mouth open without saying anything! That was it. That was all the pain I felt in the chair. Wow...I survived! (Did I get a sticker? No, she just gave me a list of instructions and told me to take four Advil® every six hours.)

Of course, I was numb for a while, but felt pretty darn proud of myself. I couldn't imagine taking so much pain medication, so I didn't. After all, I know my mouth. Then the pain set in. I was very careful not to chew of "that" side. But once in a while, it happened. My bite caused my top and bottom teeth to meet, and PAIN! I called the doctor's office. The nurse asked: "Are you taking four Advil every six hours?" Okay, I had to fess up that I wasn't following the sheet of written instructions given to me in place of a medal for being a brave patient! So, I started to follow them. Two weeks have now passed, and I can put some pressure on "the" tooth. Soon, I'll have full use of both sides of my mouth. When I tell others "I had a root canal," I get a LOT of sympathy. Folks always feel so bad. They all told me how terrible the procedure is. But when I mention it to someone who has experienced a root canal, do you know what they tell me? "Oh, it's not that bad, is it?" No, it really isn't that bad.

I now relate this experience to having your own business. People who have never had their own business are the FIRST to tell you not to do it. They give you all kinds of warnings and advice. They try to protect you from everything they can imagine going wrong. And, the incredible thing is...people listen to these "non-experienced" voices!

Like me. I had a sore tooth for nearly two years. I kept putting off going to the dentist because everyone told me how bad the procedure was going to be. But now I know differently. I wish I hadn't listened to the naysayers! Don't you, too!

Business as a Hobby

Many people tell me they began their business as a hobby. In consulting with many leaders and company management, I am asked to teach that you can move your business from being a hobby to a business. Here's my *TWIST* for you: Make your Business Your Hobby rather than simply making your hobby your business. Here are some activities of hobbyists; are you doing these activities?

1. They do their hobby for pleasure. Do you take pleasure and pride in your business, or do you feel pressured and then push others into doing business with you? Customers want to be around consultants who love their business (hobby). Why? Because when you're passionate, you can persuade others and they love it!

2. They continually learn more about their hobby. Have you invested your time into learning more about your product and how to present your product to others? Or, do you believe "this sells itself?" (By the way, "nothing sells itself"...that's a whole other subject).

3. The average hobbyist spends an average of 8 hours a week on her hobby. How much time do you spend building your business? If it's less than 8 hours, you are not making your business your hobby and your hobby is not your business.

4. Hobbyists attend conventions about their hobby. Have you ever been a guest at a hotel when a convention centered around a hobby is in session? These people are passionate enough about their hobby to gather once or twice (and sometimes even more) a year to meet others involved in the hobby and learn from each other. Do you attend your company's convention and other training sessions?

5. Hobbyists invest in the newest tools of their hobby. A true hobbyist can tell you the

best way and the newest ideas about her hobby. Can you tell your customers what's new in your business? Do you have the new products in hand to show and sell?

Your Pay Check Up

Less than a week left to go for those of us in the United States to file and pay our 2002 income taxes. This brings back a memory of my first "sticker shock" regarding taxes for my direct sales business more than 15 years ago. First of all, you have to understand that I know how to make money–but figuring out figures is not my forte'. One Christmas, my son gave me a book, *Left Brain Finances for Right Brain People*. Needless to say, the book is collecting dust on my bookshelf.

The first year I really made a substantial income in my party plan business, I received a tax bill for thousands of dollars, and I was floored! Like many direct sales consultants, the answer to not having to pay future taxes was to quit my business! Then my wise leader and good friend, Pattie, pointed out that I had to pay a lot because *I made a whole lot of money*! One reason I'm sharing this message with you at this season is to prepare yourself and your down line for tax sticker shock! If you are a recipient of this gift…consider yourself successful! You made a lot of money. Now do the *TWIST*…talk with your tax advisor and learn how to make estimated tax payments throughout the year.

With numbers in mind, you're ready to hear my tip for this week…it's quite a *TWIST* from what you're used to hearing from me. I've taught you ways to make money as you discovered how to book more parties, find more customers, hosts, and recruits. Now, I'm going to give you a pay check up—how to check up on your pay! I wish someone would have taught me this concept twenty-three years ago when I began my home party career. Instead, I stumbled upon this quite accidentally.

As soon as you set up your new business (or today) get two separate checking accounts. That's right two–not one! The first checking account will be for all your income. Key word here is "all." Meaning, if someone purchases something out of your stock–even if it's just a few dollars or less—the money doesn't go in your pocket. The money goes in the business account. All income. Leadership checks, commissions, every cent. When you have a business bill to pay, you pay it from this account. Again, all business expenses come out of this account–a real blessing at tax time! Many of you are using software programs to track income and expenses–sure makes life easier!

One of your business expenses is your personal paycheck*. For years, I used the words "You can write your own paycheck" when pitching my business opportunity. The problem is, until I began using two checking accounts, I never wrote myself a paycheck. Instead, I'd put my checks and commissions in my account, use the account for business expenses, and *pay myself as I went along*. My pay was dependent upon the balance in my business

141

checkbook. If I had money, I spent it for business or personal expenses. I figured it was mine to spend. If an expense came up, like fees for convention, sometimes I "didn't have the money to go" because I had robbed my business. Then I did the *TWIST* and set up a separate "my account" in addition to my business account.

Now, once a month (you can choose twice a month or even every week if you want; you are the boss!), I actually write myself a check for my salary from my business account and put it in "my account." Yes, I used the word "salary." Webster definition: "a fixed compensation periodically [weekly, biweekly, monthly] paid to a person for regular [other key word] work or services. You see, I am the boss of my business as you are of yours. I decide my pay rate and then figure what results I need to net this paycheck. I know that I have fixed expenses–including income taxes–that must be paid before I am paid. You might have expenses of purchasing new products, literature, and even convention and other educational fees. These are paid and put aside before you're paid. So figure what you need to do to net your desired salary.

You know how some months are more profitable than others? Well, don't increase your salary just because you have an exceptional month. Because some months are not as profitable as others and you'll need the cushion so you can depend on your salary every month/week just like you can depend on yourself to make this happen. We all know that the holiday season is the biggest in our industry. Don't spend all your profits! Rather write your own paycheck as you normally do. When you're not holding as many demonstrations from mid-December to the first of the year, you'll still be able to get your paycheck. If you do have a goal for a big month because you want to award yourself with new furniture, a pool, a car, etc., give yourself this bonus only if you have reserves in your business account. I suggest reserves of at least three months of pay.

Here's an illustration: Say you decide your salary will be $2,500 per month. You probably should figure on earning at least $3,500 per month to cover expenses (depending on your expenses, of course). Once a month you write yourself a check for $2,500! Novel idea, huh? If you only have a balance of $1,000 that month–you won't get paid. (Yes, I have had months where I did not write myself a paycheck!) Instead, work to get the results you need to bring in the $3,500. By the end of the year, you might see a substantial balance in your business account. This is a wise time to save and/or invest. Or, you might even give yourself an end-of-the-year bonus. Another novel idea! Maybe this is the time to give yourself the raise *that you've worked for and earned*—not just wished for.

Many people, when they begin a business, do not take a paycheck in the beginning so that they'll have a regular paycheck in the future. You might do this for three or four months to build up your reserves, depending on your situation, of course.

Consider this. If you were at a job interview and the company told you that your salary would depend on the profits of the business every month, would you take the position? You might think this would be a risk because you'd have to depend on the achievement of others. Let's say that you took the job and today is payday. However, when your boss explains that the sales weren't enough to meet payroll that month, how would you feel? You'd probably leave the company. Successful companies do not look at the balance in their checking accounts and spend all the money because it's there. Yet, that's how many representatives in direct sales run their finances, and when the money is not there on payday, they leave. When you have this experience in direct sales, the person responsible is the person in the mirror.

About the "my account." I put my paycheck in this account rather than our family combined account. If anyone questioned if I "made money" I had the proof–and the deposits in that account. And everything in that account was mine to spend as I wished on personal stuff— sometimes it's the mortgage! But no business expenses are to be paid from this account.

Now, I can already read your minds. You might be saying, "but my direct sales business is the sole support of my family—I have to spend everything I make." I discovered this concept when I, too, was the sole support of our family. I knew my business was the bread and butter, not the icing on the cake, for our family. I had to have a way to be sure the money was available every month. This is when I implemented this idea.

The bottom line is, people leave the business because they are not making money. Or their spouse doesn't think money is being made. When you have these two accounts, you'll have proof that you are profitable.

Activity and pay go hand in hand. Use this idea and you won't be living hand to mouth. Rather, you'll be running a business full of Sweet Successes, and Juicy Profits–and you'll be attracting other people to your business because you really are profitable and can prove it with your paycheck!

Time to check up on your pay!

*This does not imply this is a tax-deductible expense. Check with your tax advisor as to what expenses are deductible.

Persistence: Cross Lemon Aid with Chicken

We're got turkeys on our mind with the upcoming Thanksgiving holiday. That's great for a feast to eat, but if you want to have a business feast, ya gotta think CHICKEN! Yes, CHICKEN ! Most of you have eaten at a Kentucky Fried Chicken restaurant. However, you almost didn't have that opportunity. Did you know that the father of KFC, Colonel Harland Sanders, as a retired 65 year-old living on a $105 per month pension back in

1955, contacted over 1,000 restaurant owners attempting to sell his trademark secret fried chicken recipe?

You see, the Colonel owned a small, successful restaurant in Kentucky. However, when the new interstate was built, it bypassed his café. He lost his customer base and had to auction the business at a loss (sour situation!). Now, he knew he had something people wanted; he just had to find a way to get the word out. By doing the *TWIST*, he came up with the idea of selling the secret to other restaurateurs and then having them pay him five cents for every piece they sold. Easy idea.

But after traveling across the country, making DAILY (not just when he felt like it) calls, and presenting the idea to 1,008 business owners, he finally got a YES! It took him two years to get five restaurants to sign on. The man was persistent! But by 1963, 600 eating establishments were serving the famous finger lickin' recipe and the Colonel was a millionaire! JUICY PROFITS! I'm pretty sure not many of us are as down and out as Colonel Sanders was.

Did I mention he traveled cross-country in an old car that doubled as his motel at night? Even though he made chicken, the Colonel was hungry. Perhaps we have it too cushy and quit too quickly. We have other options if our business doesn't work out, we'll try something else…only to discover the "secret ingredient" for success or failure is ourselves! I recently read that the secret to our businesses is not keeping it a secret. Let's get clucking, talking, selling, sharing, and recruiting. Anytime you feel like NOT doing this, remember, we'd never have the choice between "original" or "extra crispy" if the Colonel hadn't been out opening his mouth…and spreading his wings!